PIONEERS IN PHILOSOPHY OF EDUCATION

About the Author

Mohit Chakrabarti (b. 1941) teaches Education and English at Visva-Bharati University, Santiniketan, West Bengal. Frequently participates and presents papers in National/International Conferences, Seminars, Symposia, Workshops etc. Significant participation/presentation/acceptance of papers in the World Assembly of Teacher-Educators at the University of the West Indies, Kingston, Jamaica, 1986; Beijing Normal University, Beijing, People's Republic of China, 1989; The Institute of Education, Republic of Singapore, 1990.

A translator, book-reviewer, poet and critic, profusely writes in many periodicals and research journals of repute in India and abroad.

A writer of children's books in English and Bengali, credited with more than two hundred papers, articles and creative writings.

Honoured with national award as a teacher-educator. A devoted, prolific and consistent contributor to studies in Rabindranath Tagore's educational thoughts and experiments and Gandhian philosophy and education.

PIONEERS IN PHILOSOPHY OF EDUCATION

MOHIT CHAKRABARTI
Visva Bharati University
Santiniketan
West Bengal

CONCEPT PUBLISHING COMPANY, NEW DELHI - 110059

ISBN 81-7022-566-3

First Published 1995

Mohit Chakrabarti (b.1941)

Published and Printed by

Ashok Kumar Mittal
Concept Publishing Company
A/15-16, Commercial Block, Mohan Garden,
New Delhi - 110059 (India).

Dedicated to
Professor Dwijendra Nath Ray,
My teacher.

Mr. R. Sathyamurthy,
Library Director,
United States Information Service,
Calcutta

PREFACE

Education is what man should be from the point of view of what man is. It is an endeavour - endless, creative, critical — to look within and look for the beyonding of consciousness. As such, it is a continual process of crystallization.

The centre of interest in education is the child. He has all the promise and poignance of fullness. In Rousseau : 'Child-Centric Education' this has been discussed as a focal point of Rousseau's philosophy of education.

Education as a study of the mind, and the scientific approach to education are the principal philosophical viewpoints which have been thoroughly interpreted in Pestalozzi: 'Education and the Study of the Mind' and Herbart : 'Scientific Pedagogy'.

Education by organismic evolution and auto-education—the two fundamental philosophical approaches to education as discussed in the two treatises on Froebel and Montessori may evoke newer avenues of modern contributions to the philosophy of education.

Dewey : 'Progressive Education' highlights John Dewey not only as a pioneer in dynamism in education but also as forethoughts for the educational philosophers of many more days to come .

As regards the pioneers of the East in the philosophy of education, the contributions of Rabindranath Tagore, Mahatma Gandhi and Swami Vivekananda to education through freedom and joy and through work and spontaneity vibrant with a vision for fullness of man as discussed in detail may also attract the attention of revered readers.

I would like to express may indebtendness to professor Dwijendra Nath Ray who has, indeed, baptised me in the world of teacher education. I would also like to express my sincere gratitude to Mr. R. Sathyamurthy, Library Director, United States Information Service, Calcutta, who has widened the scope for learning more on education and philosophy of the United States. I humbly dedicate this book to them as a token of my reverence.

I would also like to express my indebtedness to my wife and son who always inspire me to undertake newer and more thrilling assignments like this.

If the book serves in providing readers in general and students in particular with serene thoughts and experiments of pioneers in philosophy of education, I shall consider my work worthy and meaningful.

Seemantika
Seemanto Palli
Santiniketan - 731 235
India

MOHIT CHAKRABARTI

CONTENTS

1

PHILOSOPHY OF EDUCATION : Aims and Objectives

Education is what one should be from what one is. It is a look within to arrive at a point of looking beyond. It is also a look within to look without in the sense that it transforms and transcends one to realise one's worth as very insignificant in relation to the vast ocean of knowledge and wisdom, erudition and experience, assimilation and poignance. It paves one's avenues of excellence in expounding and exposing whatever reacts efflorescence and prepares one for a quest of newer and more thrilling avenues of erudition.

What does education do for mankind ? Is it really the most vital factor of knowing, feeling and appreciating the human mind ? Is it an intuitive process — an instinctive urge within—or a process of the continual change of the being in relation to becoming ? Is it an end in itself or a means to an end ? Is it a spontaneous urge for self-analysis, self-enquiry or self-study ? Or does it await a series of systematic, objective, fool-proof, scientific, evaluation and re-evaluational strategies for becoming of becoming with a view to renewing the onward march of the being ?

Reversely, education is also what one is from what one should be. It means a recrystallization of the ideals and objectives that mankind cherishes from time to time. It also means a continually transformed or dynamic vision of whatever enriches and advances the mind to negotiate the innumerable experiences of life. The patterns change — the patterns of life, of course, — but with the change of patterns, the mind also takes its own course. Education directs and redirects the mind in as many avenues as the learner or the teacher demands in accordance with the varying stimuli. Even when the demand remains absent or the occasion does not evolve for reasons beyond one's control, education does not, for a single moment, allow the mind to enjoy slumber. It goes on introspectively and inexpressively.

Education makes no allowance for the mind to remain in abstraction for a long time. It ceases to be what it is, when it embraces idleness and abstraction. It also ceases to be what it should be because it lacks velocity and motivation. Today's education is endangered with this dissipating tendency of being idle because it smacks of being in abstraction consequential to continual computerization in all branches of diverse manifestation. This can only be averted if education is allowed to thrive its own natural course of spontaneity and manifestation. No education becomes genuine and effective unless it is guided by an effective course of spontaneity and efflorescence.

Education allows self-analysis and self-study. If self-analysis is affected by mechanomania, education lacks mobility. It cannot play its invaluable role of self-enquiry and self-vitalization. It ignores the mind and the heart, and the exposures—inward or outward — it receives, make it passive and rather inactive. The demise of education thus committes is suicidal in nature and it indicates the demise of humanity and civilization. It is also the demise of the least possibilities of the beyonding of consciousness.

A schizophrenic society enjoying such holidays in education as hinted above is bound to encounter perils of civilization and humanism. Bereft of a sound mind and a sound heart, education becomes a blob in the sense that it faces extinction in its failure to activate the mind in the right direction. If it ignores or averts to activate the mind, it loses to bring out the inmost potentialities for self-study and self-analysis which shield man against perils of civilization and consciousness. If it does not play its part in the society to bring about a certain change of attitude towards life, life loses its charm and education, too, loses its proper role of directing and orienting civilization and humanity.

Education and Learning

Is learning an alternative to education ? Is it a factor of education that controls it? Is it always a must in case of education? These and a host of other questions veer round education and learning.

If education is a change of behaviour—a change that incorporates continuity, consciousness and caution—it includes positive or negative or a mixture of both so that it reacts to human behaviour in as diverse ways as possible. Education accommodates learning when the latter matures the former and acts as a guiding force in change of behaviour. Learning is also a kind of change depending upon the consequences of previous experiences. Unless the previous experiences so vital have no consequentialities, the education desirable remains rather inactive. That learning and education are not always equivalent and that they are complementary to each other are proved by the fact that learning through chance conditioning remains apart from learning proper and, therefore, it has hardly any significant contribution towards education. When we identify education as a sumtotal of the diverse experiences of learning — direct or indirect, distant or near, formal or informal, individual or group —it becomes meaningful and operative in the sense that it conceives and encapsulates control of learning.

Education, then, awaits a sumtotal of learning which is controlled. This also necessitates an assurance that a selection in learning is there. Otherwise, education misses the target of elimination of ambiguities and adherence to concrete items of knowledge and experience. For instance, the knowledge of the very concept of civilization incorporates manifold ideas of human civilization that covers the entire spectrum of global human behaviour with differences, diversities as well as similarities. It also incorporates the attitudinal aspects that, again, allow emotional sensibilities to play myriad roles. Now, if education is to allow localization of concept in 'civilization', it gravely suffers from numerous invaluable connotations. At the same time, if education leaves aside the points of identification of the concept of 'civilization' from a mele' of concepts and intensifies it from a controlled arena of conceptualistic approach, the identification of the concept of 'civilisation' becomes very simple and concrete, that makes education meaningful and definite in purpose.

What about other avenues of education where learning does not necessarily accommodate this controlled, straightforward simplistic strategy of negotiating multi-dimensional experience of mankind ? What is the role of the society in education where learning comes out as an inevitable and spontaneous force ? What about informal education where learning might be free from imposed control and discipline? The philosophers of education also find that control in learning is tentamount to scissoring societal contributions to education. They have arrived at a definite conclusion that milieu education, which is education through social contagion, is being continually ignored, oriented, harassed, stupified and camouflaged in erroneous learning which negates auto learning in a conventional set-pattern and welcomes fabricated learning which moulds milieu education according to needbased education. This is negative education. For instance, milieu education in the forms of traditional art, architecture, folklore etc. suffers distortion due to a certain craze for bringing at parallel levels to so-called modernity in education which twists and turns the milieu elements of learning. Sometimes milieu education, instead of being education proper, becomes, through such type of scissored learning, part education.

This is very much evident in informal learning. It is learning that loses the true connotation of learning and becomes something else than learning. It is learning that loses the 'l' out of learning and becomes totally utilitarian in its approach as it is evident in the fireworks of informal education. A crusade against illiteracy, alas, turns out to be a crusade against learning proper and degrades in merely negotiating daily drudgeries of life. Milieu education, therefore, is always a misguided education in shaking hands with informal education that is, more often than not, barely informative education and can hardly rise up to the domain of pure and perfect education.

Learning and education have a mutual bond of compromise. The greater and finer the compromise, the greater and finer is the outcome. Then, and then only, knowledge tends towards erudition and wisdom. Then, and then only, knowledge becomes an inseparable part of the whole. Then, and then only, knowledge contributes to being in addition to becoming.

Learning simply becomes a passive and mechanical factor, when dissociated from the being as the core of education and deals only with the utilitarian aspects of day to day life. In our present day streamlined education, learning becomes a prey to utilitarianism primarily because it is geared to negotiate only the day to day necessities of livelihood. Reasoning in learning enjoys holidays along with a definite absence of exercise of creative sensibilities and critical appreciation. The finer aesthetic and ethical sensibilities of life that demand an introspective and delicate exercise through learning become inoperative in the mind of the learner due to lack of exposure and exercise appropriate and desirable for defining and elucidating every point of experience. Modern education bereft of the true religion of learning is education *sans* poignance of life and vision.

Milieu Education

Weighing heavily upon factual and informational levels of education and minimising the importance of education for emotional efflorescence and synchronization have already brought down imbalance in education. Milieu education or education of the masses is severely jeopardised because the parameters of such type of education are yet to be properly re-defined. Already the appalling differences between milieu education and formal education specially from the operational, administrative, supervisional and organisational points of view are becoming wider and wider. In fact, the camps of milieu education are hardly maintaining or perhaps do not care to maintain any relationship of coherence with those of formal education, and, as such, remain isolated from or parallel to one another.

Milieu education by itself is fast removing from the basic philosophy of education that accelerates the all-round development of every individual in the society. It is rest assured and in most cases compelled to be rest assured with the second rate, lifeless, passive, mechanical type of education whereby the pupils are hardly caressed and fillipped to be on the right track or mainstream of natural or formal education. Therefore, a sense of apathy and ignorance coupled with a certain sense of abstraction and dissipation always stands in the way of milieu education that, indeed, has the only genuine spurt to highlight the true essence of education from diverse dimensions.

Milieu education is yet to be channelized for making a happy synchronization between folk culture and milieu consciousness. It degenerates into a commonalty because the basic philosophy of education in making an adventure into the world of excellence is ignored. It allows compartmentalized short-cuts to education which, indeed, affects the learners from multi-dimensional perspectives. If such education is to survive, recrystallization by means of cross-cultural and global education becomes obligatory.

To make a happy harmonization of informational, theoretical or explanatory and philosophical levels of education is long overdue in milieu education. Side by side with this, an introspective approach to personal and social ends in view of life should also be seriously taken into account.

Why Philosophy of Education?

Philosophy originates from the Greek words *Philos* (loving) and *sophia* (wisdom), which means "the love of knowledge and wisdom". Education is a casket that contains and nurtures the love of knowledge and wisdom. The philosophy of education is that love of knowledge and wisdom which paves avenues of human excellence from diverse points of view. It is, as it were, a mirror that reflects the nobler and the finer visions of life.

The parameters of the philosophy of education are best explained when the importance of philosophy in human life is thoroughly analysed. Every human being has a world of his own—a world that holds the diverse experiences of life and orients or directs it accordingly. This personal life is to be synchronized with the experiences and visions of others in and around him by means of finer involvements both in theory and in practice. One's conduct in the same way is geared within from an experience one achieves from introspective excellence. The working of philosophy thus goes on intrinsically. As Harold H. Titus significantly sums up the fundamental avenues of the importance of philosophy, which are closely related to education.

1. Each person must make decisions and act. If we are to decide wisely and act consistently, we need to discover values and the meaning of things. Life forces us to make choices and to act on the basis of some scale of values. We have to decide questions of truth and falsity, of beauty and ugliness, and of right and wrong. The search for standards and goals is an important part of the task of philosophy. Philosophy is interested in the qualitative aspect of things. It refuses to disregard any authentic aspect of human experience and seeks to formulate standards in the most reasonable way.
2. Our conduct is our own, and we are really free only when we rely upon inner controls or self-chosen ends. If a man acts as he does merely because of custom or tradition or the law, he is not genuinely free. When asked what good his philosophy did him, Aristotle remarked that it enabled him to do willingly what other man did merely because of fear of the law.
   That man is free who is the author of the principles and the laws by which he lives. In an ideal society, each person would agree with every law or, if he did not like the law, would criticize it and agitate for a change. He would do this on the basis of facts and principles which were consistent.
3. Philosophy is one of the best means to foster the habit of reflection. Philosophy can help us to change the areas of our awareness—to become more alive, more discerning, more critical, and more intelligent. In many specialized fields of knowledge there is a definite and specific body of facts, and students are given problems so that they will gain practice in arriving at the right answers quickly and easily. In philosophy, however, there are different points of view to be considered, and there are unresolved problems which are important for life. Consequently, the student's sense of wonder, his curiosity, and his speculative interest are kept alive.
4. We live in an age of uncertainty and change, when many of the

> older beliefs and ways of doing things are inadequate. Under such conditions we need a scale of value and a sense of direction. Just as we feel physical discomfort when we are in the midst of material disorder and moral discomfort when we are confronted with cruelty and injustice, so there is intellectual discomfort in the presence of fragmentary and confused views of the world.
> * * * One way we can gain unity in a world in turmoil is to achieve an inner integration, to know what to approve and what to disapprove, and to gain a sense of the meaning of human existence.
>
> Harold H. Titus : "Philosophy and the contemporary scene", Quoted in Christopher J. Lucas : *What is Philosophy of Education,* Macmillan Company, 1969, pp. 28-29

The real worth of philosophy of education is to keep oneself abreast with the deeper aspects of human life. Human knowledge and experience are, therefore, always in need of crystallization and recrystallization. Such processes are continuous and unending, and, as such, the inherent philosophy of education instils a deeper faith in humanity—a faith that reconnotates man from merely being a human being. The growth of man from physical point of view is limited in the sense that it is limited upto a certain extent but the growth of the human mind is unlimited and ever expansive. Philosophy of education ensures the unlimited growth of the mind. It encourages man to undertake and experience the adventure of life, the only adventure that beckons mankind all the time with all its infinite mystery and wonder.

To eliminate the mind of man from narrowness of the vision of life, philosophy of education acts as a supreme force. As ignorance leads to confusion and apathy to disintegration, the intrinsic value of philosophy of education lies in waging a crusade against ignorance and apathy. Know the mind as you know yourself is the *sine qua non* of philosophy of education. In this respect, it represents as a pivotal force of self-purification by means of endless self-askance and self-enquiry. Am I what I should be in terms of others far and nearby me ? Am I responsible for my every action and contemplation though ostensively insignificant ? Am I responsive to the inner call of conscience or consciousness ? Am I justified to the universal truism so serenely voiced forth by the Upanishad: *sa vidya ya vimuktaye* — that which emancipates is learning? When education embraces this philosophy of the inner vision of mankind, it justifies its aura of effulgence so vital to the fulness of man *par excellence*.

Philosophy of education is not only a critical analysis of the deeper vision and meaning of life, but also a process that aims at two very important aspects. These are: (a) analysis and (b) synthesis. While analysis is concerned with the clarification of the diverse problems of education, synthesis has its parameters in supplying us with possible alternatives.

Keeping in mind the above aims and objectives of philosophy of education, the philosopher of education cannot be assured with the theories of education for the sake of theories alone. Rather are these theories dependent on their appropriate applications in defining and explaining by him. As such, the philosopher of education highlights philosophy of education from the following avenues of performance:

(a) Identification, analysis, and evaluation of other areas of specialization directly or indirectly associated with philosophy of education.
(b) To be justified to philosophy of education as a resource-person covering the areas of specialization.
(c) As an inter-disciplinarian, the philosopher of education looks at the minute points of affinities and departures among different disciplines and probes deep into the points of cohesion.
(d) To determine the policy perspectives of philosophy of education by specially encompassing teacher education for cultivation and advancement of philosophy of education.
(e) To unfold manifold avenues of research in philosophy of education by undertaking projects on creativity, values and so on to eliminate isolation from the greater and wider canvas of life.

Philosophy, in the true sense of the term, is a part of the human quest. If this is so, it cannot avert the influence of education upon it. As such, the synchronization between philosophy and education is the only way to negotiate the quest for what is best for mankind. Life to be worth living must find its meaning both in philosophy and in education. The marriage of knowledge and experience as education and philosophy truly suggest can only be saved from irrelevance when they are saved from isolation. As Bertocci elucidates,

> A philosophy of education is not a description of what is being done in the educational process at any given time. It is an attempt to evaluate as systematically as possible, in the light of human experience

> and knowledge available, what the aims and presuppositions of educated living are. A philosophy of education is not, first and foremost, a philosophy of schooling in a given society or state. Why? Because we cannot take for granted that any particular society or system of schooling is motivated by aims consistent with the nature of the life good to live (to use Kilpatrick's phrase) in this kind of universe. Yet what differentiates philosophy of education from its close neighbours, ethics and social philosophy, is not its neglect of either but its more specific focus on the total educative process.
>
> The aim of a philosophy of education is to help human beings become fully conscious of what is involved in evaluating the direction of their experience with a view to the life worth living. With this backround, I say unblushingly that unless philosophers become educators and educators become philosophers both philosophizing and educating lose living contact with the underlying human need, to know what is dependable in persons and their universe, and to live in accordance with their findings.
>
> In a word, the divorce between "philosophy" and "education", like many other divorces, created more problems than it solved. It left both partners with a threatening, if not actual irrelevance to the fundamental human question: "What life is worth living, what learning is worth undergoing, in this kind of universe ?" Thus, the philosophers who left the "Cave" of education and forgot to return escaped the derision of the cave-dwellers only to be disregarded and to feel, at critical moments, like interesting parasites even on the back of the academic community. The educators who never made the ascent were always in danger of unshackling prisoners from their chains but still leaving them among the shadows of life, about which they, now unchained, could talk more glibly.
>
> — Peter A. Bertocci : "Unless Educators Be Philosophers, And Philosophers Be Educators", Quoted from *What is Philosophy of Education ?* by Christopher J. Lucas, The Macmillan Company, Collier-Macmillan Limited, London, 1969, pp. 292-293.

To determine the aims of education in relation to philosophy is to determine the points of synchronization between life and society, education and values, education and the individual and the individual with national and global consciousness. Here, for the model, the purpose in each item is determined to be of any value in accordance with the value it embodies in relation to philosophy of education.

The problem of philosophy of education starts with the cohesion of philosophy and education put together. The elementary matters of life make a significant influence on education that awaits everyone's involvement. The field of enquiry for cause and effect relationship allows happy but really challenging avenues of education which for innovation and justification to every individual's sense of inquisitiveness demand the positive role of philosophy.

The common approaches to defining educational philosophy are to regard it as a point of view and an application of philosophy to education. Added to these is to regard philosophy as the generalised theory of education. In the first place, when educational philosophy stands for a point of view of education, the individual finds an avenue to look at himself and look within through education. This is, indeed, desirable in every human action and contemplation. Secondly, when educational philosophy is defined in terms of regarding it as an application of philosophy to education, the responsibilities of education are perhaps greater. Education then turns into a philosophy of life in relation to human involvement by means of knowledge and experience. A study of philosophical systems in connection with education becomes all the more encouraging and stimulating to an individual because the different theories of philosophy like those of idealism, realism etc. become living and exciting in terms of education for human involvement with these theories. As regards the approach to defining educational philosophy as a generalised theory of education, the task of the educator becomes all the more significant as an educational philosopher. Here he not only conforms to the demands of philosophy in education to negotiate the diverse problems as such, but also applies philosophy to interpret education by utilizing theories, techniques, methods and principles thereto.

To define philosophy of education in terms of social life as suggested by Dewey allows involvement of philosophy in education as a practical approach to exercise insight and freedom in reflective thinking. This definition ensures acceptance of different hypotheses to be evaluated from time to time. As Dewey suggests,

> Freedom of thought denotes freedom of thinking; specific doubting, inquiring, suspense, creating and cultivating of tentative hypotheses, trials or experimentatings that are unguaranteed and that involve risks of waste, loss and error. Let us admit the

> case of the conservative; if we once start thinking no one can guarantee where we shall come out, except that many objects, ends, and institutions are surely doomed. Every thinker puts some portion of an apparently stable world in peril and no one can wholly predict what will emerge in its place.
>
> — John Dewey : *Experience and Nature,* p. 222.

To welcome philosophy in education is to welcome good sense and sensibilities. It is not only desirable to understand and appreciate the meaning and purpose of education but to have an indepth analysis of the content of educational practice. It is high time that all our educational endeavour should be geared towards both these ends-in-view. The philosophy of subject-matter will, then, come under the preview of content in education. To implement such as end-in-view of education, the suggestions put forward by Hall-Quest as a design for philosophy of education are invaluable :

1. The revision of present courses whereby much of the present content will be deleted and a wholly new content substituted in its place.
2. A wholly new course, entitled "The Philosophy of Subject Matter" might be organized within an expanded department of educational philosophy. This new course would be a fusion of the meanings that underlie the subject-matter of public education.
3. The department of the philosophy of education might become the core of the school of Education and in and through it all other departments might be philosophically interpreted to the end that the student may see the many interpretations of what he doubtless now views as a loose aggregate of courses in Education that lack cohesive unity in a programme of teacher preparation. Such a fusion would include all courses in educational method and student teaching.
4. Between the school or college of education and other departments of the college or university a cooperative arrangement might be evolved whereby these other departments would offer in their respective fields interpretations of professional value for teachers, such interpretations to be derived through a reviewing board composed of representatives of the various interests concerned.
5. A wholly new course in the philosophy of education might be

taught by a number of professors from various fields, the course continuing through the year and each instructor responsible for a four or six week's unit, the course as a whole to be directed by the professor of the philosophy of education.

6. A series of lectures by subject-matter specialists might be planned, such lectures to conform to the design of the series as philosophical in the sense used in this discussion and each lecture based on a mimeographed or printed syllabus with bibliography; credit value to be allowed on the basis of intensive study of the philosophy of subject matter in the student's subject matter speciality.

— Alfred L. Hall-Quest: "Design for Philosophy of Education", *What is Philosophy of Education?* by Christopher J. Lucas, The Macmillan Company, Collier-Macmillan Limited, London, 1969, p. 229.

If every teacher is a philosopher, every point of learning contributes to the philosophy of education. As such modern philosophy of education widens its parameters to different disciplines to develop an inter-disciplinary approach to philosophy of education.

The taxonomy of today's philosophy of education, therefore, stimulates diverse avenues of learning outcomes which lead to the ultimate end-in-view of fulness of man as represented in the following table.

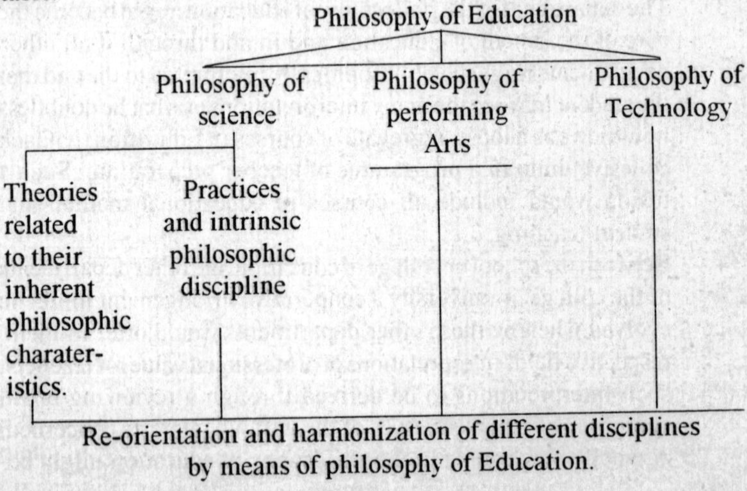

As philosophy of education is concerned with "the predicaments, the prospects, and aspirations of men", so characteristically referred to by John Dewey, it has its focal point of the Socratic dictum : "Know thyself". A very difficult task, indeed, for everyone to be true to the dictum, there is a certain possibility of falling in line with tradition which betrays the essence of individuality. This leads us to the vital role of philosophy of education : to bring about a certain sense of awareness and self-consciousness in man through education.

Admittedly, a sound philosophy of education well implemented or nursed with caressing attitude by means of self-consciousness often serves as a fitting reply to all confusions and ambiguities even where sciences fail to negotiate. It also enables to be emancipated from allegiance to conformity and conformism which often detrack humanism. Philosophy as such has its own pattern of efflorescence often shaking hands with eccentricism but it is undeniable that philosophy of education is a distinct answer to anachronism or ambiguities by means of radicalism in practice and poignance.

To discover the bearings of both philosophy and education on the criss-cross of value commitment and to find out the ideal avenue of conflict resolution through a comprehensive and synchronized theory of human values are long overdue. The task of philosophy of education is to create a common platform of understanding and appreciation of diverse disciplines. In fact, the role of philosophy of education is like the role of a disseminator of clear, specific, pin-pointed exposures of knowledge and experience in its endless laboratory of education. As Dewey rightly suggests, "Education is the laboratory in which philosophic distinctions become concrete and are tested."

What are the probable outcomes of the laboratory of education in relation to philosophy ? In the first place, philosophy of education, is an interesting activity to be justified and clarified with metaphysics, ethics and epistemology. The factual part of education is indeed closely related to metaphysics which explains each item of knowledge and experience in terms of its appropriateness or inappropriateness and often plays the role of enriching and supplementing with finer exposures. Secondly, what education recommends as a reasonable principle or guideline for a concept to be aimed at, ethics lends a helping hand in providing clarification and justification to it. Thirdly, a theory of learning well-nourished in epistemology strengthens it to be worth application in boarder and more intricate perspectives of human endeavour.

The role of the teacher in understanding philosophy of education and applying it in actual class-room situation is legion. It is he who creates and re-creates an introspective vision through dissemination of principles of education well-baked in the fire of poignance of philosophic vision. The finer points of humanism are enkindled through his very exposure to every item of learning for his pupils. Added to these are the ethical, moral, spiritual and aesthetic values which contribute a lot to the fulness of education as well as of philosophy in a well-balanced content and method of education.

If education aims at excellence, philosophy of education aims at greater excellence the pursuit of which is not only desirable but also mandatory to the teacher. To kindle the lamp of every child deserves that pursuit—untiring, endless, thrilling.

Is our education in unison with philosophy ?

2

ROUSSEAU : Child-Centric Education

Education, to be true to its meaning and purpose, must begin with the child. It must place the child at the centre and orient diverse programmes for the all-round development of the child.

An incomparable exponent of child-centric education, Jean Jacques Rousseau wages a war against rigour and discipline in the name of education of the child so long nursled in the earlier part of the eighteenth century. A period of stagnation as this century might be branded, it endeared dominance of arbitrary control, authority, discipline, orthodoxy and rules and regulations only to thrust the mind of the child in its course of education to be duped in autocracy. The revolt that brought about a definite pattern of change in the education of the child against all odds during this century was primarily steered by Rousseau and Voltaire.

Rousseau ardently believes that children should enjoy freedom in thought and action, learning and contemplation. They should be saved from the rigour of teaching. As he suggests with poignance, the real development of the child in course of education is self-development. This means that every child should be allowed to be a child and be protected from being polluted by artificial and passive education received from teachers or others interested in his teaching. Let him be allowed to learn what he needs to know. Let not the present be sacrificed at the altar of the future of the child in education because the future, as Rousseau thinks, will take care of itself.

The challenge of education is the challenge of the inner self. Rousseau, therefore, allows the child to be natural in his course of education. He may be allowed to enjoy spontaneity in development and prepare himself to face any experience and eventuality of life by means of self-understanding, self-appreciation, self-dependence and self-development. A forerunner of pragmatism as he really is, he rightly understands the ills of the education of the eighteenth century that make children victims to conservatism and orthodoxy in the name of education, and plays the role of a reconstructive revolutionary in the education of the child. As Power observes,

> Even if his (Rousseau's) ideas proved to be unsound, they would, he was confident, stimulate good ones among his readers. The point he wants to make is this : more should be known about children. They should be studied and educated as they are, rather than for what they are expected to be as adults. The great error of the age, Rousseau claimed, was to regard children as small adults, never considering what they are capable of learning. Obviously, Rousseau did not think himself an expert in child psychology, and only after much persuation did he revise the first drafts of Emile to include a discussion of infant years. As it was he anticipated future developments in child study and suspected others would follow the trail he marked out. If Rousseau had done nothing more than enter a plea for an understanding of children, he would have made a lasting contribution to the business of education.
>
> —Edward J. Power : *Evolution of Educational Doctrine: Major Educational Theorists of the Western World,* Appleton-Century-Crofts, New York, 1969, pp. 279-280.

The father of child-centric education, Rousseau first declares education as one's birth-right. Let the floods of the light of education, as he strongly advocates, be allowed to flourish everywhere in the mind of the child in the midst of Nature who is the supreme teacher and not in the caged, walled, camouflaged class-rooms and closed nurseries. A revolutionary in education, he stimulates the development of the 'noble savage' in the child and intensifies the iconoclastic spirit dormant in every child. An undaunted and non-conformist visionary in education, he holds out the inner philosophy of modern education in his inimitable and vibrant language as follows:

> Pressure the child within a condition of dependence upon things alone; this is the way in which you can follow the course of nature in his education, oppose nothing against his indiscreet desires but the physical obstacles they must overcome and the punishment

> which his own actions will bring about and which he will recall on similar occasions in the future so that, without forbidding him to refrain from wrong doing, he will, nevertheless, be prevented from so doing. His experience or his importance will serve in place of the observance of law. Take no heed of his demands, provide only what he needs.
>
> It is then not a question of obedience when he acts or of tyranny when you act for him. So he will come to know equally what it is to be free in his actions and what it is for you to be free in yours. Supply only that power on his behalf which he requires for freedom and not for imperiousness so that he receives your assistance with some humiliation and seeks to dispense with it the moment he can aspire to serving himself without assistance.
>
> — Jean Jacques Rousseau : *Emile,* Translated by Barbara Foxley. Everyman's Library Series, Dent. p. 49.

Like a devoted naturalist, Rousseau believes that the spontaneous growth and development of the child in the midst of Nature is the best form of education. Indeed, the key-note to his philosophy of education is referred to in the very beginning of his epoch-making book *Emile* :

> Everything is good as it comes from the hands of the Author of Nature; man meddles with it and deteriorates.
>
> —*Ibid.* p.5

The theories and principles of education as Rousseau propounds are not detached from his personal life and experiences. Born on June 28, 1712 in Geneva, he received a rude shock in the education of life itself when he loses his mother just after ten days of his birth. His father, a watch-maker and unbalanced person faces trouble from the Genevan authorities and leaves the city abandoning Rousseau under the care of his aunt. The most fragmentary training in schooling as he receives during this period is at cross-roads with livelihood that leads him as a vagrant youth. The two years of attachment to the office of a notary followed by a search for occupation as an apprentice to an engraver proves to be futile. But the otherwise scholastic minded Rousseau shows his love for reading — a quality nursled within himself like a romantic passion for enjoying literature more and more — by selling his shirts to buy books while serving as an apprentice to an engraver.

Deeply attached to Catholicism, Rousseau comes in contact with Mme de Warnes who becomes his protector, mistress and tormentor and whom he considers an authority like a loving and erudite mother. Meanwhile, at 17, he feels within himself that his true metier is music and so he studies music for six months under Lemaistre, an expert teacher in music. He seeks his lot as an opera musician in Paris in vain, returns to Mme de Warnes, is baptized as a Catholic in Turin, takes service as a lackey, learns Latin and returns from a seminary within two months to the latter only to renew the relationship after ten years as a lover even though there is a difference of age between Mme de Warnes and him of twelve years.

Aimless and bohemian as Rousseau is by nature, he switches over from the job of a tutor, seeks funds for publishing his novel system of musical notations, presents the work before the Academic des Sciences in vain and then publishes himself in January 1743 only to be betrayed in fame and fortune. This year, of course, he accepts the post of secretary to the ambassador in Venice, which faces the same fate of longevity like his apprenticeship to an engraver. Two years later he marries Therese Levassier, stays with her for the rest thirty-five years as a life's inseparable partner but suffers from a brooding sense of failure as a consequence of his ambition and declining hope. His contact with Diderot, a philosopher of eminence, provides him with an opportunity to contribute an article on music in the *Encyclopaedia,* but the controversial issues on religion by Diderot are a curse for his lot as Diderot is arrested and imprisoned. Rousseau regularly visits Diderot in prison only to be encouraged continually to write an essay in order to participate in the competition on the role of science and arts in the changing patterns of morality. This brings forth success for him, which inspires him later to seek entry into another essay competition in December 1753 on 'What is the Origin of Inequality amongst men and is it authorised by the Natural Law?.

Ill and worried, Rousseau takes refuge in writing. Both fame and denunciation are parts of his genre. But finally he is forced to lend himself into extreme poverty and ill health. An epoch ends with his death in 1778 at Ermonville. The slogan of the French Revolution hailing the spirit of liberty, equality and fraternity with the fillip of a born revolutionary, Paris honours him with his remains transferred from Ermonville.

According to Rousseau, education depends on the role of three teachers in cooperation with one another. They are Nature, Man and Things. While we have control over the last two, the first one is beyond control. As such, the education of the child should have close conformity with Nature. To allow the child to respond to Nature in education is the only way to restore and stimulate spontaneity and originality in education and life. What Rousseau thinks about the role of Nature in the education of the child is an outcome of his concept of natural, enjoyable, living, harmoniously balanced, useful, sympathetic and unrepressive methods of education for child development. Observation of Nature, therefore, becomes an essential factor in education. As he characteristically observes,

> Observe nature and follow the way she traces for you ; she is ever urging children to activity ; she hardens them by presenting them with all kinds of difficulty ; she teaches them very early what it is to suffer and know grief.
>
> — *Ibid.* pp. 14-15

To face any eventuality in life is the most prized lesson that we, as Rousseau believes, receive from Nature. He also discourages use of medicine which he considers a betrayal of faith in Nature and overdependence upon one of the 'fashions' of the society :

> For myself, I do not know of what ills we are cursed by the doctors, but I do know that they infect us with many deadly maladies; cowardice, faint-heartedness, credulousness and fear of death . . . . Medicine is all the rage these days and no wonder. It is the diversion of indolent and unoccupied people who do not know what to do with their time and pass it preserving themselves . . . Such people as they require the doctor who will flatter and threaten them and give them the only enjoyment to which they are susceptible — that of not being dead . . . (Just) as I will have no call for doctors myself I would call none for Emile unless his life was in evident danger, for then the doctor could be no worse than kill him.
>
> — *Ibid.* pp. 21-22

Rousseau also discourages insistence of artificial habit formation for the child but instead, he advocates 'natural habits' of the child to be developed independently and not guided by established habits. In his words,

He wishes to touch and to handle everything; do not oppose him in his restlessness for it provides him with a vital apprenticeship . . . It is only by movement that we apprehend what is of ourselves and that which is not of ourselves, and it is only by our own movement that we acquire the idea of distance. Lacking this idea the infant indiscriminately reaches for objects approximate to him and those a hundred paces away.

— *Ibid.* p. 44

The negative education that Rousseau indicates about the education of the child is based on the theory that he learns where no one teaches. He gets worthy dividends from the capital of his sensory experience which is never guided by any precept from the teacher as such. 'The new born infant is straightaway a pupil not a tutor but of nature' (*Ibid,* p. 28.) Rousseau, therefore, allows total freedom of development of child with all his activities in the ideal atmosphere of Nature who is his only teacher. As he warns,

> Do not restrain the child from the moment it first draws breaths. No caps, bands and swaddling clothes. Let him be garbed in loose fitting clothes which leave his limbs at liberty and are neither too heavy so that they check his movements nor so warm that they prevent the air having access to him. Place the child in a wide, well padded cradle within which he can move with ease and safety. When he grows stronger, allow him to crawl about the room; let him develop and exercise his little limbs and you will see him gain in strength daily. Compare him with the child who has been tightly confined in swaddling clothes and the differences in rate of progress will astonish you.

— *Ibid.* p. 45

It is interesting to note in this connection how Rabindranath Tagore as an educationist comes closer to the views of Rousseau in allowing children to be natural with Nature and discouraging the evil habits of dresses that hinder their appropriate growth and development. The degeneration of everything into the hands of man as Rousseau suggests has its appeal to the educationists at least due to the fact that the child is allowed a natural atmosphere where he finds the most positive avenue of efflorescence of his personality. The spirit of self-dependence also develops from the education that the child receives directly from Nature.

Conventional or formal education thus replaced by Rousseau through natural and positive education has been warmly received by later celebrated educational philosophers.

To guard a teacher against the 'pedantic mania for teaching, as Rousseau observes is the first condition of education of the child. Let him be allowed to initiate himself in the world of learning alone. Away with the usual practice of teaching and that is the right method of teaching the child in allowing him to the practice of self-teaching. The job of the educator is to draw out 'perfact' man from the child in course of discharging duties like a midwife. As Rousseau significantly elucidates,

> Before human prejudices and human institutions have impaired our natural inclinations the happiness of both children and adults consists in the use they make of their liberty but the liberty of the former is limited by their own weakness. Whoever does so as he wills is happy if he is self-sufficient and this is the condition of man in a state of nature. He who does as he wills is not happy if his desires exceed his powers as is the case with children in a state of nature. Even in this state then, children enjoy only an imperfect liberty similar to that enjoyed by grown men in social life. To the extent that any of us are dependent upon others we are to that extent weak and wretched. We were intended to grow to be men; laws and the dictates of society plunge us back into infancy.
>
> —*Ibid.* p. 49.

The restlessness of the child is the green signal for its positive role in being active in education. Rousseau, therefore, emphasizes on utilizing Nature towards this end-in-view to have the experience of liberty and abundance of life,

> Nature strengthens the body and allows for growth by her own means and one's only care is to do nothing to thwart this. One should never require a child to be still when he wishes to move about nor to move around when he wishes to remain still. When the child's will is not impaired by our shortcomings then they wish for nothing that is not useful. Let them leap, run about and shout as much as they wish. All their movements serve the needs of their constitution if it is to be strengthened. However, one should be distrustful of such desires as they cannot themselves fulfil and which must be answered for them. Always one must distinguish with care the true, the natural need,

> from the fantasy need, the acquired desire from that which comes from the abounding life I have spoken of.
>
> — *Ibid.* p. 50.

No verbal lesson, as Rousseau advises, should be imparted to the child. Instead, what he thinks of utmost importance to the child for his growth is to encounter diverse experiences of life. Neither punishment nor moral suggestions should be given to the child as these would be detrimental to his ability to exercise independent power of thinking. In the words of Rousseau,

> Give your pupil no kind of verbal lesson at all; he should receive nothing but experience. Inflict upon him no sort of punishment because he does not comprehend what it is to be at fault, and do not require that he begs your pardon for he does not understand what it is to give offence. Not yet having a capacity for moral judgment he cannot be said to act immorally and so merits neither chastisement nor reprimand. I can imagine that the frightened reader will immediately compare this child with others; he will be mistaken in his judgment. The continual control put upon these children excites their vivacity—the more they are constrained when under supervision the more they are turbulent the moment they can escape; they make every effort to compensate themselves for the restrictions you place upon them. ..... I believe you will have achieved much if you have managed to hold your tongue.
>
> — *Ibid.* p. 56.

To hold one's tongue in case of education of the child as Rousseau advises, is the key-note of his viewpoints on child-centric education. As education is life itself and not a preparation for future state of life he insists on making a harmonious relationship between the experiences encountered by the child and the life to be led for complete living. The aim of education should, therefore, be complete living. How to initiate the child in the education of complete living ? Rousseau's answer is to allow the child to negotiate certain types of hardship in course of enjoying freedom of thought and action. As he observes,

> I see the little rascals playing in the snow, blue and benumbed, scarcely able to move their fingers. They could take themselves off

> to a warm place but they do no such thing; if one compelled them to do so they would be a hundred times more conscious of hardship than they are of the rigours of the weather.
>
> Do you imagine that true happiness is possible to anyone who is not acting according to his nature, and is it not contrary to the condition when one removes from the situation all the misfortunes to which the species is naturally subject ? I would say that if one is to experience the great goods one must experience also the small misfortunes; this is his nature. Too much bodily comfort corrupts morals. The man who knows nothing of pain and sorrow can know nothing of compassion nor of the sweetness of commiseration ; his heart could be touched by nothing, he would have no social sense, he would be a monster among men.
>
> — *Ibid.* p. 51

Rousseau whole-heartedly believes that education is a development from within, and so, the child should be allowed to develop by himself the innate capacities. The vast resourceful world of wisdom and experience is the only great book for him to learn. Only facts are necessary for him to learn and whatever instruction is to be given is only to be directed as a means to an end and never an end in itself.

The duty of one interested in the education of the child is primarily to actively and sincerely play the role of a gardener. Children are, as Rousseau thinks, nothing but plants. As plants require appropriate and careful cultivation for their normal growth and development, children in the same way await good education in the three-fold avenue: to shield them against all corruptions, to cultivate their sense of duty and to enable each of them to cultivate and develop the body and the mind by means of careful and cautious exercise of the sense organs. When Rousseau speaks on negative education he emphasizes on losing time rather than saving time as one of the most fundamental rules of education. Accordingly, not to instruct in virtue or truth but to preserve the heart from the vice and the spirit of error becomes the end-in-view of education of the child. As he significantly submits,

> May I make so bold at this point to reveal the greatest, the most important, the most useful rule of all in education ? It is not that one should save time but that one should lose it. The ordinary reader must pardon my paradoxes; they are unavoidable when one thinks for oneself and, whatever you might say, I prefer to be a man of paradox

> than of prejudice. The most dangerous period of human life is that between birth and twelve years of age. It is the time when errors and vices germinate and there is yet no instrument for their destruction. When the instrument is available the roots are so deep that it is too late to tear them out. If children sprang straight from their mothers' breasts into the age of reason than the usual form of education would be suited to them, but the natural progress requires an altogether contrary approach for there to be in accord between growth and education.
>
> —*Ibid.* p. 57

Not to reason with the child but to allow him to develop his own reasonings is as Rousseau thinks the surest way of serving growth in education. While children respond to their 'immediate reasoning and perceived interests' they seek freedom from unnecessary thrusting of knowledge and interest in matters on the future of manhood and/or matters alien to them. What is really important in case of education of the child is to allow him to exercise his own faculty of reasoning rather than to be guided by the reasoning of his teachers or others who fail to honour his own reasonings. As Rousseau characteristically remarks,

> Nevertheless I am far from thinking that children posses no sort of reason. On the contrary I notice that they reason very well in all things that have a bearing upon their immediate and perceived interests. But it is on the extent of their understanding that people are misled so that they are attributed with knowledge they do not have and so urged to reason about that which they do not comprehend. Yet another mistake they make is to attempt to turn the attention of children to considerations which in no way affect them, such as interest in their futures of their happiness when grown to manhood and the opinion of people will have of them when they are grown up; talk which, when directed at those quite unpossessed of foresight, has absolutely no significance. Now all the enforced study of these poor wretches concerns subjects which are utterly foreign to their minds. You must judge how much attention they are able to give to them.
>
> —*Ibid.* p. 72

Earlier, Rousseau categorically states that the principal aim and objective of education is not to hinder but to serve and promote growth in children:

> As they have no wish or thought to make the child a child but a university scholar, most fathers and teachers feel it can never be too soon to correct, reprimand, cajole, threaten, induce, instruct and reason. Do better than this; act reasonably and do not reason with your pupil. Above all, do not force approval of what he actually dislikes because in this way reason is constantly associated with distasteful things so that it becomes distasteful to him to reason before he is even able to understand what it is to use reason. Exercise his body, his organs, his senses and his powers but keep his mind idle for just so long as you can. .... Finally just what lessons are really necessary to him? Guard against giving today that which could be deferred until tomorrow without danger.
>
> —*Ibid.* p. 58

Sense-development which is so essential for the education of the child is also the central point of interest in Rousseau's philosophy of child-centric education. He insists on nursing of the sixth sense of the child, which he spells out as follows:

> This sixth sense is not dependent upon a particular organ; it resides nowhere but in the mind and its sensations, which are purely internal, and called perceptions on ideas. It is by the number of these ideas that our knowledge is assessed; their distinctness and clarity determine accuracy of thought and the art of comparing one with another is what is called human reason. Thus what I term childlike or sensory reason consists in the formation of simple ideas by the combination of several sensations, and what I call intellectual or human reason consists in the formation of complex ideas by the combination of several simple ideas.
>
> —*Ibid.* p. 122

Education, as Rousseau elucidates, is life itself. We are actually educated in three ways viz. Nature, Man and Things having close cooperation with life; otherwise education loses its main purpose in the life of man. The first lesson for the child is, therefore, the lesson of how to live, and live by the urge to live that comes from within. He requires no guide than himself. Rousseau's *Emile* has rightly been characterised as the gospel of childhood from this end in view.

As regards education for value-orientation, Rousseau supplies us with invaluable maxims in the education of the child. The finer sensibilities thus exercised by the child contributes a great deal towards education for fulness. As he instructs,

> Do not let your pupil form the habit of looking down from the height of his pride upon the sufferings of the unfortunate, the labourings of the miserable, and do not hope to teach him to consider them in others if he considers them as foreign to himself. Make him well aware that the condition of these unfortunates can be his own; that a thousand happenings may plunge him in a moment, unexpectedly and inevitably, into all their unhappiness. Teach him to take no account of birth, health or torture; show him all the vicissitudes of chance.
>
> —*Ibid.* p. 185

Quite aware of how to deal with the young and the adolescent, Rousseau harbours more on honouring the exercise of individuality than on sermonising by the teacher. Absence of control of the adolescents by the teacher indicates absence of showing respect to the adolescents' own vision of thinking and negotiating every aspect of human life. This has been clearly exposed when Rousseau remarks:

> Teachers complain that the turbulence of this age makes the young ungovernable, and I observe this; but is it not the case that the teachers are at fault? As soon as this energy has been allowed to flow through the senses do they not understand that it is not possible to divert it? Will long, cold sermonisings by pedants efface from the mind of the pupil the memory of pleasures he has conceived, banish from his heart desires which torment him, kill the ardour of a temperament that he knows how to use? Will he not batter himself against the obstacles which oppose him in the only happiness of which he has an idea? In the harsh law imposed upon him without his understanding how could he not see the caprice and hatred of people who seek ways to torment him? Is it strange that he rebels and hates everyone about him? I am well aware that, by being rather easy, one makes oneself tolerated and can keep an apparent authority, but I cannot see at all the value of an authority which is only

> maintained over a pupil by fomenting the vices it should prevent; this is to calm a fiery horse by making it leap over a precipice.
>
> Far from the energy of an adolescent being an obstacle to his education, this passionate involvement is that which brings it to consummation and achievement; it is that which can win for you the prize of a young man's heart when he ceases to be less strong than you are. His first affections are the reins by which you direct all his movements; he was free but I see him reduced to servitude. So long as he loved nothing he was dependent upon himself alone and his own needs; as soon as he loves he is dependent upon his attachments. Thus he forms the first ties with his species. * * * * * It is not until after his natural self has been cultivated in a thousand ways, after much thought about his own feelings and those he observes in others, that he can succeed in generalising his individual notions under the abstract idea of humanity and unite with his own individual affections those which may unite him with his species.
>
> — *Ibid.* p. 194

To involve the child in doing good deeds is the first lesson on socialism and humanism that the teacher can sincerely impart. Rousseau, therefore, gives practical suggestions for orientation of the child towards exercise of social virtues as follows:

> You believe you are teaching your children how to live when teaching them certain bodily contortions and certain formulas of speech which signify nothing.
>
> I also believe that I have taught my pupil how to live because I have taught him to live with himself and, more than that, to gain his bread. But this is not enough. To live in this world he must know the ways to influence them; he must calculate the action and reaction of individual interest within a society and foresee their outcomes so accurately that he is rarely foiled in his enterprises or will, at least, always adopt the most appropriate means towards success. * * * The exercise of social virtues affects the heart deeply with the love of humanity; it is through the doing of good that we are made good; I know of no surer way. Occupy your pupil in all the good deeds which are within his power in order that the interests of the poor are as if his own, that he assists them not only through his purse but with his labour; that he serves and protects them; that he dedicates to them his person and his time; that he acts as their agent; he will not have

so noble an employment in his life.

— *Ibid.* pp. 211-212

Rousseau's child-centric education cannot avert the following points of criticism:

(i) By isolating the child from the society, Rousseau allows the child to be anti-social.

(ii) By allowing too much freedom of individuality, Rousseau encourages the child to be indifferent to and ignorant of the opinions and viewpoints of others. Again, this autocratic attitude and extreme point of independence also ignore the value of reading books and gaining information and knowledge from those books.

(iii) Purely theoretical and sentimental, and never practical and realistic, Rousseau's child-centric education fails to keep pace with contemporary theories and practices in education.

(iv) There are innumerable and strange inconsistencies in Rousseau's philosophy of child-centric education. His *Emile* is, as Voltaire scoffs, "a hodge podge of silly wet nurse in four parts".

(v) Rousseau remains incomplete and fragmentary in his approach to education of the child. He is simply a visionary and so he rests himself assured with introducing and setting everything on fire without finding out an appropriate solution to the problems of education. In fact, he invents nothing even though a critic like Lanson considers *Emile* a fragrant asphodel and evaluates it as "the most beautiful, the most thorough, and the most suggestive treatise ever written".

Even though vituperations against Rousseau beat down like sheets of rain, it is undeniable that the course of his thoughts and principles of education is like that of an ever flowing river with numerous branches. As a forerunner of modern education it is he who inspires Pestalozzi in the education of sense-training and physical education, stimulatings Herbart to deal with curiosity and interest as motivational factors in the education of the child, and impresses Froebel in nurturing motor expression.

Over and above all these psychological movements in education, it is beyond doubt that the educational philosophy of Maria Montessori is entirely dependent on the basic aspects of Rousseau's philosophy of child-centric education.

Centuries will wane away and, in the meantime, many more educational philosophers will contribute to the education of the child but Rousseau will ever remain like a guiding star ever glowing with the halo of brilliance in revolutionary thoughts on education of the child for better efflorescence.

REFERENCES

Rousseau Jean Jacques, *Emile*, translated by Barbara Foxley, Everyman's Library, Dent, London.

Broome J. H., *Rousseau : A Study of his Thought*, Arnold, 1963.

Green F. : *J. J. Rousseau : A Critical Study of his Life and Writings*. Cambridge University Press, 1955.

Power Edward J. : *Evolution of Educational Doctrine : Major Educational Theorists of the Western World*, Appleton-Century, New York, 1969.

3

PESTALOZZI : Education And The Study Of The Mind

More a social philosopher than Rousseau, Pestalozzi is, as it were, interested more in ploughing the furrows of human imagination and talking directly to school-masters to make them aware of the study of the mind of pupils. He wants to convince them of the fact that schooling has actually missed the mark for it is entirely directed towards the education of the affluent and the advantaged, leaving aside the interests of the poor and the disadvantaged in schooling.

Sensing the utter frustrations and denial of education in case of the poor, Pestalozzi revolutionalizes education as an instrument of social change and economic betterment. Strictly humanitarian in his approach to education, he is action-minded and experimental. Even though he is the author of a novel entitled *Leonard and Gertrude,* and a concoction of aphroisms as expressed in his work *Evening Hours of a Hermit* written a year earlier in 1780, the germ of his pedagogic credo finds favourable ground in dealing with the innovative and psychological methods of teaching. The initial hypothesis with which he launches his philosophy of education in practice is that man, by nature, is good but the society often deprives him of the manifestation or exercise of goodness. Therefore, what is of primary importance in education is to ameliorate degrading social circumstances. This will definitely lead to progress in education. But how to reform society? Pestalozzi prescribes the training of the child for social living through natural education.

Born in an ideal home of upper middle class family in Zurich in January, 1746, Johann Heinrich Pestalozzi loses his father, a physician at the age of six. His mother, a very sensitive woman, brings him up in a secured atmosphere at home. But his youth as he thinks has made him a stranger for he 'did not live in the world in which (he) dwelt'. Highly sensitive, imaginative and intelligent, he is often misinterpreted during his youthful days by his friends and others who consider him poorly coordinated and without any practical experience. He does not think his schooling meaningful and effective because he strongly believes that formal education is in most cases equivalent to a colossal waste of human endeavour and talent. At sixteen, he comes across Rousseau's *Emile,* reads its eight hundred pages with great interest and attention and develops the spirit of pedagogic ambition by keeping Jacob, his first-born, close to Rousseau's Emile in experimental designs. From vain efforts at studying law to farming at Neuhof, an experiment to last in futility for five years, he switches over to writing to ventilate his dogged struggle in living as he elucidates, "in the midst of fifty little beggars, sharing in my poverty my bread with them, living like a beggar myself in order to teach beggars to live like men". Thereafter as a school teacher at Stanz for two years he only kisses failure as his revolutionary experiment on elementary education for the orphans greet the French troops to occupy the building without opposition. At fifty two, he is a teacher again at Bergdorf where his experiments on education have drawn worldwide attention. But this silver lining in his career as an educational innovator is erased in the more powerful halo of politics in 1803 when the Bergdorf castle is requisitioned. Frantically, Pestalozzi now moves at Hofwyl to continue his experiments on education in collaboration with Emmanuel von Fellenberg, his close associate and admirer who finally deserts him. Two years later, Pestalozzi reopens his institution for preparing prospective teachers at Yverdon. Here he climbs to the apex of his fame. For long twenty years he enjoys the faith of all interested in education. Then, again, doubts and dissentions take the upperhand in the midst of the members of the staff in his own institution which faces closure in 1825. He seeks asylum in his old Neuhof haunt and two years later he expires.

With a penetrating and warm wisdom steered to the well-being of mankind Pestalozzi always loves and understands man in spite of his sentimentalism at times expressed in his romantic vision of education for the disadvantaged. In the preface to the first edition of his semi-autobiographical novel *Leonard and Gertrude* he frankly remarks, "I take no part in the disputes of men about opinions, but I think all will agree, that whatever makes us pieces, good, true, and brotherly, whatever cherishes the love of God and our neighbour, and whatever brings happiness and peace into our houses, should be implanted in the hearts of all, for our common good."

Pestalozzi's viewpoints on natural education is mainly developed on the principle of harmony between educational practice and the natural process of development of the child. In terms of pedagogy, he develops and explains this principle with the following terms of reference :

(i) Education should be continual and synthetic. It should be liberal in its approach and embrace numerous branches of knowledge and experience. It should be a positive force to the development of mental abilities and maintain a coherent, relevant and continual approach to learning;
(ii) Education should regulate and penetrate the entire human being. It should never be lifeless, dull, mechanical, superficial, partial and passive; on the other hand, it should be living and pulsating, active and spontaneous, complete and natural;
(iii) Education should liberate the mind of the child. It should allow ample scope for exercise of innate capacities of every learner to develop his individual character in as best a way as possible. Such form of education is positive and natural because it admits individual differences among children and allows individual endeavour for cultivation of innate faculties of manifestation;
(iv) To facilitate grading of students and learning materials, education should be progressive, continual and graded. No learning gap should also be entertained in the education of the child;
(v) Education should nursle morality and religion. It should always keep close relationship with God, which is a fundamental principle of natural development of the child;
(vi) Education should be practical. Pestalozzi pays greater attention to relevance in his concept of practicality than to any other point and emphasizes on the means of development from the actual conditions of life; and
(vii) Learning of the child must begin from his own level of experience. The experience, again, must be direct. Hence, the importance of intuition in education, which ensures distinct, foolproof, clear and specific perception of learning subjects.

Pestalozzi's method of teaching aims at four objectives:

(i) to enable the child to make a close contact with reality;
(ii) to ensure meaningful perception on the part of a child;
(iii) to ensure the child of fulness of understanding; and
(iv) to develop the innate faculties of the child and enable him to execute in a worthwhile manner that incorporates both the active as well as the passive power of the mind.

The most distinctive item in the pedagogy of Pestalozzi is his theory of mental productions where he delivers his methodological manifesto of teaching as follows:

> I thus concluded that the art of educating our race must be based upon the first and simplest results of these three fundamental elements - Sound, Form and Number; and that instruction in anyone department could and would never lead to a result beneficial to our nature, considered in its whole compass, unless these three simple results of our fundamental faculties should be recognized as the universal starting-points for all instruction, fixed as such by nature herself; and unless these results were accordingly developed into forms proceeding universally and harmoniously from them, and calculated efficiently and surely to carry instruction forward to its completion, through the steps of a progression unbroken, and dealing alike and equally with all three. This I concluded the only means of proceeding in all three departments, from indistinct intuitions to definite ones, from intuitions to clear perceptions, and from clear perceptions to intelligent ideas.
>
> Thus, moreover, I find art actually the most intimately united with nature, or rather with the ideal by means of which natures make the objects of the creation known to us; and so was solved my problem, viz., to discover a common origin of all the means of the art of instruction, and, at the same time, that form of it in which the development of the race is defined by the constitution itself of our nature — and the difficulty removed, in the very way of applying the mechanical laws, which I recognize as the fountain of human instruction, to that system of instruction which the experience of thousands of years has given to the human race for the its own development; that is, to writing, arithmetic, reading etc.
>
> —J. H. Pestalozzi : *Leonard and Gertrude,* in Henry Bernard, *Pestalozzi and His Educational System. pp*. 676-677.

Among the factors of mental processes, Pestalozzi gives priorities to the following in the exercise of intuition:

(i) The powers of considering unlike objects in relation to their forms and of recalling to mind their material;

(ii) The powers of abstracting these objects as to their number; and

(iii) The power of repeating by language, and fixing so as not to be forgotten, the conception of an object as to number and form.

— *Ibid.* p. 675

The source of all human knowledge that Pestalozzi hints at is five-fold. This five-fold source deals with impressions derived from things, the guidance received form parents and teachers, independent endeavour, the results of our activities involving labour and effort, and with the ways and means analogous to our knowledge derived from intuition. In his words, the sources of knowledge, therefore, are the following:

(i) through the impressions derived from things around us, when brought into relation with our five senses;
(ii) through whatever is brought before our senses by the intervention of methodic guidance, so far as this depends upon our parents and teachers;
(iii) through our own determination to attain to knowledge, and to obtain intuitions by our independent striving, after the various means of them;
(iv) through the results of effort and labour in our callings, and all activity which has not mere intuition as its object; and
(v) through a means analogous to our intuitional knowledge; in as much as it instructs us in the properties of things not pertaining properly to our intuitions, but in which we perceive a similarity to things which we know by our intuitions.

— *Ibid.* pp.689-690

Even though Pestalozzi admits that memory plays a vital role in the education of the child, he prefers to individual ability to express on the basis of his personal experiences. The goal of learning is primarily dependent, as he thinks, on teaching on the elementary levels by the teacher who encourages the learner to repetition in a selected area. Every aspect of learning is thus treated as discreet and in the final analysis the work of collation in goals is taken up for execution. No new aspect of learning should be taken up prior to this activity.

How does Pestalozzi explain his own method of instruction? Here is the answer in his own words :

> My method of instruction is distinguished especially in this, that it makes use of language, as a means of lifting the child from obscure intuitions to intelligent ideas, than has heretofore been the case; and also in this, that it excludes from the first elementary instruction all combinations of words which presuppose an actual knowledge of language. Any one who admits how nature leads to intelligent comprehension of all things by a clear comprehension of a single thing, will admit also that single words must be clearly understood by the child before he can intelligently comprehend them in connection; and any one who admits this, rejects at once all the received elementary books of instruction ; for they all presuppose an acquaintance with language in the child before they communicate it to him.
>
> — *Ibid.* p. 687

Why does Pestalozzi give maximum emphasis on object-training? The training of the senses, as he thinks, depends on how one trains the senses of pupils through exercises in observation. The method to be followed in this connection for the education of the child has also been specifically spelt out by Pestalozzi as follows:

(1) Instruction is by actual inspection.
(2) Proceed from the easy to the difficult.
(3) Go from the known to the unknown.
(4) Go from the near to the distant.
(5) Go from the simple to the complex.
(6) Go from the concrete to the abstract.
(7) Instruct according to the nature of the material but also according to the nature of the child; thus, give in each hour, if possible, a little whole in content and form.
(8) Use poetry in the service of instruction.
(9) Use conversation.

— *Ibid.* pp. 201-203

To introduce the psychological foundation in the education of the child is, therefore, one of the landmarks in Pestalozzian philosophy of education. What Pestalozzi actually strives for in the education of the child is to observe beneath the surface of those psychological principles that are concerned with learning. Added to these principles are the natural avenues of development of the child replacing artificial ones that are both abstract and ambiguous in elucidating ideas for better understanding and appreciation. As a forerunner of Rousseau, he does not claim anything novel or extra-ordinary in his vision of educational reconstruction. In fact, in his vision of eliminating the chaos in education and in bringing about a positive change in neglected and degraded humanity, he frankly admits his indebtedness to Rousseau for the epoch-making viewpoints expressed in *Emile.* As he writes in his *Swan Song,* "My own visionary tendencies are stimulated to a pitch of extraordinary enthusiasm when I read that dream book of his. I compared the education which I had received at home and at school with that which Rousseau demanded for *Emile,* and I felt how wretchedly inadequate it had all been." The point of departure that Pestalozzi seeks from Rousseau, and actually makes so, is to make the negative and general principles of Rousseau concrete and positive. As such, he does away with negative education by replacing artificialities through psychological methods and principles of education.

Sympathy with the child by means of a study of the nature of his mind makes Pestalozzi's philosophy of child-centric education really appealing and interesting. The psychological movement of education as the great Swiss school-master introduces, for the first time brings about a radical change in approach to the intellectual, moral and physical development of the child in the process of education. What he sincerely deserves, as he himself is kind, pious and self-denying, is to enlarge the scope for home affections in the school. The genial family environment with which he is blessed in his own life leaves in his heart a profound and excessive confidence in mankind to win over sufferings and constraints of life. As he admits in *Views and Experiences,* "From childhood it lay in the peculiarity of my character and of my home training to be benevolent and kindly and to have unlimited confidence in those about me. I came early into association with the suffering and the poor, and in a thousand experiences with them, came to feel the deepest sympathy with them and their many sorrows; and I likewise came to feel the urgent call to attempt to improve the multifarious causes of the evils which they endured". This, indeed, brings Pestalozzi close to the grossroot level of the society.

To psychologize education, Pestalozzi feels the urgent need for socialization of education. The road to right action as he thinks, lies in right thinking, right feeling and right living. So he urges on the necessity of self-development of the individual for the betterment of the society. When he speaks of the natural, progressive and harmonious development of the powers and capacities of each and every individual, he primarily emphasizes on the fact that education is the birthright of all.

Education of the child to be an individual and social being in the truest sense of the term must, as Pestalozzi thinks, be ensured with living and sincere sympathy with which his heart is touched to be true to his character morally, socially and intellectually, and must be stimulated with self-activity and self-confidence. His poignant suggestion to the teachers as written in his novel *Leonard and Gertrude* is : "You should do for the children what their parents fail to do for them. The three R's are not, after all, what they most need. It is all good and well for them to learn something but the really important thing for them is to be something. When this truth will be fully realized by teachers and school managers, there will be some hope for national education." Not merely to learn but to be is, therefore, the core of Pestalozzi's viewpoints on education.

To delve deep into the child's inborn faculties is one of the basic principles of Pestalozzi's philosophy of education. Accordingly, the work of the school-master is to make education begin in the child and work from within outwards. Thus, the work of the school-master is primarily to emancipate the child from stifling of individuality under a pressure of borrowed contents. Let the child be allowed to follow the teacher as his guide in observation. Creativity in him will, then, automatically find its avenue of manifestation.

However, the prescription of Pestalozzi in observation by the child for learning fails to avert the possibility of stifling his mind with a mass of facts. Who denies that in such a process of observation, object lessons in the absence of a proper guide become dull and drab, forcing the child to be mechanical? As Professor Meyer remarks,

> Observation...... became the basis ofPestalozzian instruction. Guided by the questions of his teacher, the child, observing an object, proceeded step by step from what was perceptible to his senses to the generalizations which lay beyond. In Pestalozzi's deft hand the procedure became a creative act. Fashioned from the thing before the eye, and illuminated by a fine fancy, the lesson began to glow with a freshness it had not known before. It was in this respect a work of art— and one in which the old man outshone many of his imitators who, though vastly more systematic and learned, lacked his buoyancy and, even more, his inner warmth, and thus reduced the object lesson to a perfunctory cant. In sad truth, as the years ran on, the object lesson, like the old-style recitation, became just another way of stifling the child with a mass of facts.
>
> —Adolphe E. Meyer: *An Educational History*

of the Western World, McGraw-Hill Book Company, New York, 1965, pp. 358-359.

Even psychologizing education as Pestalozzi visualizes cannot avert ambiguities both in theory and in practice. His very concept of teaching reading for children suffers from the maladies of rote learning and abstraction. Drawing, in his concept of teaching the child, unnecessarily and unscientifically becomes a primary factor in observation, where it precedes the latter. Again, hand-writing becomes a subject of drawing in his pedagogy, that affects the psychological processes of learning how to write and how to draw.

> Pestalozzi wanted, as he said somewhat cryptically, "to psychologize education", by which he meant that the pupil should begin his learning with simple things, and as he became their master, move to the more and more complex. Unluckily, in the half light of a primitive psychology, Pestalozzi's sparing acquaintance with the workings of the mind often played him false. What tripped him was his delusion that what was simple to him was also simple to the child. In consequence, as Pestalozzi undertook to simplify what the youngster was to learn, he sometimes unwittingly did just the opposite. Take reading, for example. To strip the business to its simplest terms, sawed words down to their barest combination, which is to say, a vowel and a consonant, as witness, ab, eb, ib, and so on through the entire alphabet. These pairs, which he marshaled into a collection known as "syllabaries", and which ran to a large number, the pupil was made to learn before he was allowed to introduce himself to actual words, and in due time, sentences and paragraphs, and on some remote tomorrow, books.
>
> Although Pestalozzi generated a great heat on behalf of observation, he did not, like Rousseau, let the learner draw freely from what he saw. Like reading, drawing was first rolled into the dissecting room where Pestalozzi anatomized it into its barest elements. Consequently, before the child was put to sketching, say, a house or a cowshed, or even the flaming sun over an Alp, he was made day in and day out to practice on curves, angles, and lines, vertical, slenting and horizontal. In the same manner hand-writing became a subdivision of drawing. Letters, separated into their component parts, were found to contain elements which were bent, sloped, or straight, some running up and down. These the budding pen-man was set upon in long and arduous rehearsal before he was trusted to try his hand on

actual letters, followed in course of time and practice by words, sentences, paragraphs, and cantos.

— *Ibid.* p. 359.

Pestalozzi believes that the values of memorization in the education of a child are legion. To achieve more complete knowledge he stresses on memorization of names by the child. The advantage gained, as he believes, is "immeasurable in relation to the facilitation of subsequent instruction", but recognition, identification of qualities apprehended and the desirable distinct expression in relation to number and form by the child remain far outside the perview of Pestalozzian philosophy of education. As Power characteristically observes,

> Memory plays an exceedingly important role in the system, and Pestalozzi is entirely content with this. But what he is getting at is that an ability to express oneself must begin on the level of the most immediate personal experiences. When the child is able to express himself clearly and distinctly, it is time to introduce grammar. This is done in order to achieve the last purpose of instruction in language, rendering intelligent ideas; but the whole process, despite the brave beginnings toward reconstruction of methodology, is at best dissatisfying, for Pestalozzi has actually done little more than assert that the basic natural principle of learning is repetition. In a sense, he is saying, teaching on the elementary levels should employ repetition selectively, that is, goals should be determined and kept discrete until each part of learning is mastered.

— Edward J. Power : *Evolution of Educational Doctrine : Major Educational Theorists of the Western World,* Appleton-Century-Crofts, New York, 1969, p. 304

Admittedly, the principle and practice of education nurtured by Pestalozzi has a fundamental basis of love and humanitarianism which are the essential components of religion. The seeds of love and humanism sown by means of cultivation of domestic education along with intellectual education will, as he believes, lead to purity of mind and broadened vision. The relationship between the teacher and the child at school should be the same as that between parents and the child. Again, while the child should regard his teacher like his parents, he should also regard his class-mates in the school as his brothers and sisters. This harmony of relationship through education leads to understanding and appreciation to religion and morality. But it is undeniable that morality and religion await practical approaches to be exercised through education and Pestalozzi is not clear in his programmes for moral and religious education, if any, for the child. As such, moral and religious instructions are not desirably amalgamated in his programmes on education,

> Throughout Pestalozzi's writings there is much talk about harmony in the development of the child; Pestalozzi never tires of stressing his doctrine that man is a moral, intellectual, and physical being and that there should be harmonious relationship among these three dimensions. In the final analysis, Pestalozzi would have selected the moral (and religious) side as most in need of careful development, although he is enthusiastic for the physical and intellectual, because he always entertained a clearheaded and uncomplicated approach to man's relationship to God and to the fundamental dependence men have on God. This much is clear in his total philosophy of life, so we are surprised to find that his school methods are not very elaborate when they treat of moral and religious education. No doubt Pestalozzi expected much moral training to occur in the home, and large portions of this training were the work of informal and incidental education, but the school played its part too. His school program for religious education is in no way separate from moral formation; thus both are to be formed by the same instruments. The specific ways that education may promote virtue, goodness, and piety are offered quickly and without extensive justification, probably because Pestalozzi saw no need for justification. Such education begins with pious exercises, the principle of which is prayer; and includes, in addition, religious conversations, wherein the distinctions between earthly life and heavenly and everlasting life are presented to the child in a clear and practical manner, the study of sacred history and the *Bible,* and, finally, religious instruction "properly so called; or the regular explanation of the doctrine of our Savior". Formal religious instruction did not appear early in the educational program—probably not before age fifteen-but, as a whole, education was always religiously oriented, and this basic plank in Pestalozzi's platform should dramatize his independence of Rousseau's agnostic pronouncements.
>
> — *Ibid.* pp. 305-306

A practical educational thinker and practitioner, Pestalozzi realizes that education should not be entirely left alone at the mercy of Nature but it should be psychologized and conformed to Nature. Herein he makes a definite point of departure from and improvement upon Rousseau. He goes a step ahead of the latter's theory of individualism and places the child in the midst of the society for desirable social synchronization. For this, he advocates positive and concrete education.

Glorified with rare honour in 1792 as a "Citizen of the French Republic" and knighted in 1814 by Tsar Alexander of Russia, Pestalozzi has one, all embracing aim — to restore human dignity by means of appropriate dissemination of education and awaken the sense that a good state begins with good individuals. He also instils the spirit of regeneration of individuality after the Swiss Revolution of 1799 for liberation of masses and encourages through practice in performance to develop strength and virtue in every individual. His philosophy of social regeneration, indeed, serves as a milestone in the history of human civilization and global excellence of mankind. Here is a statement of appreciation by a visitor, a temporary companion or Pestalozzi:

> I have seen more than the paradise of Switzerland, for I have seen Pestalozzi, and recognized how great his heart is, and how great his genius; never have I been so filled with a sense of the sacredness of my vocation, and the dignity of human nature, as in the days that I spent with this noble man, I cannot think without emotion of this little company of brave men, struggling with the present that the future may be better, and finding alike their joy and their reward in the hope they have of raising children to the true dignity of humanity.
>
> — Roger De Guimps : *Pestalozzi : His Life and Work,* Appleton-Century-Crofts, New York. p. 263.

The words engraved on the bust of Pestalozzi in the city of Brugg in the Swiss canton of Aargau are :

> Here Rests
> HENRY PESTALOZZI
> Born in Zurich, the 12th of January, 1746 Died at Brugg, the 17th of February, 1827 Saviour of the poor at Neuhof and Stanz, father of orphans at Bergdorf and

Munchenbuchsee, founder of the popular school at Yverdon. The educator of humanity; man, Christian, and citizen. All for others, nothing for himself. Peace to his ashes.

TO OUR FATHER PESTALOZZI
Grateful Aargau

When comes such a dedicated personality in education?

REFERENCES

Frost, S.E.: *Historical and Philosophical Foundations of Western Education,* Charles E. Merrill Publishing Company, Columbus, Ohio. 1966.

Kilpatrick, W.H. : *Heinrich Pestalozzi : The Education of Man,* Philosophical Library, New York, 1951.

Meyer, Adolphe E. : *An Educational History of the Western World,* Mc Graw-Hill Book Company, New York, 1965.

Power, Edward J. : *Evolution of Educational Doctrine : Major Educational Theorists of the Western World.* Appleton-Century-Crofts, New York, 1969.

Silber, Kate : *Pestalozzi: The Man and his Work,* Routledge and Kegan Paul, London, 1960.

Walch, M.R. : *Pestalozzi and the Pestalozzian Theory of Education,* Catholic University of America Press, Washington, 1952.

4

HERBART : Scientific Pedagogy

An illustrious name in the method of education, Herbart combines in him the philosopher and psychologist. His main purpose in education is to establish scientific pedagogy. His principles of education are essentially an elaboration of the educational principles of Johann Heinrich Pestalozzi, his teacher and forerunner who has christened him in the process of instruction in education. The initial points of departure from his teacher include more accurate and vivid observation, clarification and analysis of the system of education and viewing the mind not divided into several watertight and specific compartments as the faculty psychology of Aristotle denotes but as a unity or continuity that embraces a uniformity of diversity or unity in plurality. He also makes a significant departure from earlier educational thinkers, except Kant in his theories on education, as the first educationist who makes the foundation of education upon phychology. As a positive thinker of scientific pedagogy, he rightly thinks that the world of education for the child should be directed towards observation, proper application of the sense and paying attention to every concrete and simple idea in the arena of knowledge. These would certainly ensure elementary education a success.

Born on May 4, 1776 in Oldenburg, a city in north-west Germany, Johann Friedrich Herbart is the only child of a highly ambitious, dominating, energetic and intelligent mother and successful lawyer father. At five, he falls into a tub of boiling water, and as a result of this serious injury, passes the rest of his life in a delicate constitution. He receives his early education under the guidance of his mother who herself becomes his constant companion in learning till he is ten years old. From twelve to eighteen years he is a student at the Oldenburg gymnasium. At fourteen and seventeen, he writes an essay entitled "Concerning the Doctrine of

Human Freedom" and delivers a lecture on "The Commonest Causes that Affect the Growth and Decay of Morality in various States" respectively. He studies philosophy for three years at the University of Jena where he makes intimate friendship with Schiller.

After graduation Herbart becomes the tutor of three sons of the governor of Interlaken, Switzerland. During this period he visits Pestalozzi who initiates him into the world of pedagogy. At twenty-six he completes his doctoral thesis in philosophy and within a short span of six years, he writes three important books on pedagogy and philosophy. His most remarkable glory in life comes at the age of thirty-three when he adorns the chair of philosophy, so long occupied by Immanuel Kant, his mentor, at the University of Konigsberg, East Prussia. It is really for him a fulfilment of a long cherished dream. As he remarks,

> How happy I was to receive the offer of this, the most renowned chair of philosophy, the place which, when a boy, I longed for in reverential dreams, as I studied the works of the sage of Konigsberg.
>
> — Quoted in *Historical and Philosophical Foundations of Western Education* by S.E. Frost, Charles E. Merrill Publishing Company, Columbia, Ohio, 1966, p. 381.

In his twenty-four years of distinguished and illustrious service at the University of Konigsberg, Herbart plunges himself deeply on philosophy and psychology. During this period, he contributes abundantly to both these disciplines, and at least four books prove how mature and sharp he is in both theory and practice in philosophy and psychology. The later years of his life is dedicated to the continual and devoted endeavour in the theory and practice of education in particular at Gottingen where he dies of a stroke on August 14, 1841. "He entered," as Professor Meyer observes in benign respect, "eternity, so as to say in cap and gown a day or so after having committed his last lecture."*

A "scholar's scholar" as he has been rightly described, Herbart ventilates his pedagogical poignance and practical experience in the opening lines of his work *The Science of Education : Its General Principles Deduced from Its Aim:*

> The aim of all those who educate and demand education is determined

---

* Adolphe E. Meyer : *An Educational History of the Western World,* McGraw-Hill Book Company, New York, 1972. p. 366

by the range of thought they bring to the subject. The majority of those who teach have entirely neglected in the first instance to construct for themselves their own range of thought in view of this work; it opens out gradually as the work progresses and is formed partly by their own characteristics, partly by the individuality and the environment of the pupil.

—J.F. Herbert: *The Science of Education: Its General Principles Deduced from its Aim,* (Tr. H.M. and E. Felkin) Quoted in Edward J. Power: *Evolution of Educational Doctrine: Major Educational Theorists of the Western World,* Appleton-Century-Crofts, New York, 1969, p. 311

What Herbart wants to emphasize in education is not in its theories alone but essentially on the practical aspects of thrilling experiences. His main concern in education is to eliminate obsession in practice and aware teachers to be aware of the importance of on-the-job training. He neither repudiates the educational thoughts of earlier thinkers like Locke, Rousseau and Pestalozzi nor does he claim any innovation in educational philosophy, but what he feels and actualizes in practice is the application of the theories of education in practical teaching. In fact, to bring theories down to the level of practice is one of the most salient contributions of Herbart in his scientific pedagogy. As Power elucidates,

> Herbart does not argue that educational theory is inoperative or non-existent; he was too good a scholar, too much in touch with the literature in education to have allowed himself this questionable luxury. In various places in his own writings he makes pointed, and often extended, allusions to other educational theorists. Locke, Rousseau, and, of course, Pestalozzi are paid special heed. So the point of his remark is not that theory is ignored. He complaints that theory is not brought down to the level of practical teaching issues, that theory too often, in fact almost always, remains on an antiseptic level and affects neither the mind of the teacher nor the practices he employs. This would not do, Herbart believed, because education was not a theoretical but a highly practical question; teachers needed dependable information about goals and processes before they entered the classroom. Too much valuable time and human talent were allowed to waste away while teachers decided, or determined

in their on-the-job training, what they should do and how to do it.

—Edward J. Power: *Evolution of Educational Doctrine: Major Educational Theorists of the Western World,* Appleton-Century-Crofts, New York, 1969, p. 311.

As an educationist *par excellence,* Herbart is primarily concerned with the two most important questions. These are : (a) What is the fundamental goal of education? and (b) What does schooling mean? As his philosophy and psychology are the basis of his educational theory, he insists more on developing 'esthetic taste' freely and consciously among children who may possess strong character and become good men and women in future. The role of the teacher is neither to directly instruct nor teach morality but to accelerate the 'many-sidedness of interest' in them through a presentation of multi-dimensional range of experiences.

Herbart is always interested in the method of creating interests which exist, as he thinks, in the positive relationships of ideas in the mind. How is an idea born? According to him, it is born out of the contact with the 'Soul-Real' or Ego with another real. What should be the teacher's role? As he instructs in the classroom, he is in fact, absorbed in the mind of each of his pupils. His instruction turns into construction. He controls the environment of the child. At the same time, he determines the interests, will and character of the child. In so doing, he plays the role of a builder of the child's mind.

The foundation of education in values as Herbart seeks, is based on the following five principles :

(i) The principle of the idea of equity

This is a principle that elucidates the principle of justice. According to this principle, Herbart asserts that virtue should be rewarded and vice punished. The practical role of virtue in education makes the latter more meaningful in life than in the practice normally undergone through instruction in education. Moreover, the role of morality and ethics as defined and practised by Herbart makes pupils more responsible for honesty, integrity and appropriate action and protects or safeguards them against unethical deeds.

(ii) The principle of the idea of justice

This principle as a pre-requisite to the principle of the idea of justice shows how Herbart develops and practices it in terms of the general idea of justice and its relation to social demands and social responsibilities. Mere conforming to social forces with regard to justice would lead to doubts, discrepancies and delimiting the rights of an individual.

(iii) The principle in relation to the concept of inner freedom

This principle, as Herbart elucidates, ensures a marriage of insight and volition. In education, he pays attention to the development of moral insight. Absence of moral insight affects a clear concept of inner freedom which should be differentiated from external influence. Herbart also suggests the role of the teacher in identification of insight and volition on the part of a pupil. This will definitely enhance the spirit of morality in the latter.

(iv) The principle of the idea of perfection

Herbart also calls this principle as the principle of the idea of efficiency. It is entirely based on the aesthetic view of the world as Herbart substantiates in his philosophy of education. It advocates nursling of a strong will by the learner. The constituent components of a strong will, as Herbart explains, are concentration, intensity and extension. While the former two are purely individualistic and are hardly controlled by external forces effectively, the latter comes under the perview of education in boosting moral and intellectual development. Let the child be allowed to exercise resoluteness, determination and stick-to-itiveness by means of appropriate and desirable schooling. Then, the strength of the will on the part of the child would automatically emerge. Presumably, Herbart wants to safeguard the learner against the forces of bad will and immorality in action.

(v) The principle of the idea of benevolence

This principle as Herbart asserts enables the learner to identify, analyse and apply the different patterns of what is good to himself in relation to the good of others. He, of course, does not want that the teacher should always be on the alert in practicising what is good to his pupils as it may prove unsatisfactory and even a failure. But he is certainly inclined to a pattern of the value system by means of following this principle.

Herbart comes closer to Locke's theory of *Tabula Rasa,* when he psychologically thinks that the mind is a 'clean slate', 'a blank tablet' 'an empty sheet of paper' or 'a dark chamber' which indicates that it indicates nothing innate or intuitive at birth. Perceptions-external and internal-penetrate into this clean slate of mind. Herbart orients the theory of Locke by maintaining that the mind relates itself to the environment through the nervous system. With primary presentations of sense-perceptions the consciousness of ideas is born to manifest those ideas into experiences. As a teacher one should work with experience and intercourse in order to see that the pupils react with primary presentations which might lead first to the process of conception and generalisation and then to that of reasoning and judgment.

Herbart's famous theory related to the psychology of apperception or apperceptive masses brings forth a new avenue of educational plans and programmes for development of the child in thinking, reasoning, formulating new ideas and inferences and evolving specific viewpoints. The association of ideas as indicated in his psychology of apperception is nothing but a joining of new ideas with the old. As Ivor Morrich characteristically explains,

Each experience is a presentation to the individual; a presentation which may become a permanent element of his awareness and comprehension of his environment. His mind is, or becomes, an interrelated collection of presentations, or apperception mass. It is the function of the mind, or soul, to receive, classify and relate experiences, or ideas based upon experience.

Presentations, then, are the basic elements of mental life, and their combinations, permutations and interactions are the cause of all forms of consciousness. The interactions of the 'empty arena' of the pure soul with the external world produce derived presentations, which in turn comprise the greater part of the mind's contents. These, in their turn, can play their part as representations, which form the material for the higher processes of thought. The masses of presentations in the mind (apperceptive masses) derive from experience and intercourse. It is from experience that the teacher seeks and helps to create knowledge, and from free intercourse sympathy. Apperceptions are, basically, the assimilation and identification of a new idea by the mass of ideas already in the mind. Herbart used the term 'idea' to include sense-impressions as well as intellectual and emotional impressions.

> Contrary to the theory of Locke, ideas were for Herbart both active and operative forces. Some ideas, or presentations, are contrary, or opposite, and so diminish each other, because they are mutually exclusive. Some ideas are similar, or compatible, and so they retain their intensity and a fusion takes place. The new presentation has greater strength than either idea regarded separately. Other ideas, again, may be disparate; that is, they do not conflict, nor do they fuse, but they remain members of a mass or complex. An object, for example, may be identified as an orange; it is, in fact, an apperceptive mass with presentations of colour, shape and smell which are neither in conflict nor in fusion. Thus Herbart developed, and gave a certain dynamism to, Associationist psychology, with laws of similarity, contrast, disparity, contiguity, and so on.
>
> — Ivor Morrish: *Education Since 1800,* George Allen & Unwin Limited, London, 1970, pp. 183-184.

Admittedly, the principle of Apperception is the most significant doctrine of Herbart's whole system of education. Along with this, his method of correlation is also another characteristic feature in making a fusion between one subject and the other to make them mutually dependent and related for better understanding and appreciation of both. With correlation, Herbart also gives emphasis on his doctrine of concentration which also plays a very significant role in the science of education. By this doctrine, he asserts that one should entirely devote one's attention to a single act of thought. This enables one to grasp a particular concept clearly and completely and correlate it to other subjects as well. As Eby analyses these two doctrines of Herbart,

> By "concentration" he (Herbart) meant the complete absorption of the attention in single acts of thought; it is that mental experience by which the mind is wholly immersed in a single idea to the exclusion of every other interest. It is the focusing of one's whole consciousness upon a single object of thought.
>
> The disciples of Herbart have given a broader application to the term. They regard "concentration" as the grouping of all studies in the curriculum around our common central study. Such a central subject might be evolution, around which Biology, Physics, Geology and other sciences would be correlated. For elementary education, History, Geography, Literature, or manual activities have been used

by different theorists as centers. Herbart himself looked upon the ethical enlightenment of the youth as the central process of education. History and literature are the dominant means, while nature study and mathematics are subordinate.

Such a central core is necessary for several reasons. First, the number of studies that press for a place in the curriculum is too large to treat each of them with equal fullness. Second, the unity of the mental life requires that there be a unity in the knowledge of the individual. Third, * * * the ethical life is the unifying principle of the soul.

"Correlation" is the process which accompanies concentration. It is this process that makes one subject central, but sees to it that each topic studied receives full support from all other objects. For example, in connection with the discovery of America, history and geography may well be assisted by drawings and maps and by facts taken from nature, literature, and even arithmetic. These two doctrines, concentration and correlation, have played a large part in forming our conception of the scientific educational method of instruction.

— Frederick Eby: *The Development of Modern Education,* Prentice-Hall of India Private Limited, New Delhi, 1964, p. 491

Herbart's "scientific educational method of instruction" has been further accentuated by the five Formal Steps popularly known as Herbartian steps. To formulate a method of instruction, these steps, as Herbart asserts, are essential. These are :

(1) Preparation
(2) Presentation
(3) Association
(4) Generalization
(5) Application

All the five steps referred to as above, are termed as 'clearness' for preparation and presentation, 'association' for comparison and abstraction, 'system' for generalisation and 'method' for application. Again, the last three steps have been described by the other Herbartians as assimilation, application and recapitulation respectively. We can also interpret 'application' as Herbart actually aims at, by the term 'evaluation.'

However, it is better to listen to Herbart's own explanation as stated in *The Science of Education* on clearness, association, system and method as follows:

> Quiescent concentration if it be but clear and pure, sees single things distinctly. For it is only clear when everything is kept at a distance that makes the act of presentment a turbid mixture, or when several varied concentrations disintegrated by the teacher's care are presented one by one.
>
> The presentations are associated by the progress of one concentration into another. In the midst of the crowd of associations hovers imagination; it tastes every mixture and despises nothing but the tasteless. But the entire mass is tasteless as soon as the elements can commingle with one another, and that is possible only, if the clear antithesis of single things does not prevent it.
>
> Quiescent reflections see the relationship of the many; it sees each particular thing as a member of the relationship in its right place. The perfect order of a copious reflection is called system. But there can be no system, no order, no relationship without clearness in single things. For relationship does not lie in mixture, it exists only amid separated and re-united parts.
>
> The progress of reflection is Method. It runs through system, produces new members of it, and watches over the result in its application. Many use the word who know nothing of the thing. The difficult business of cultivating the mind according to method must be on the whole left to the teacher.
>
> — J.F. Herbart: *The Science of Education,* pp. 126-127. Quoted in Edward J. Power: *Evolution of Educational Doctrine: Major Educational Theorists of the Western World,* Appleton-Century-Crofts, New Delhi, 1969, p. 330.

To shape the school master's approach to education, these Herbartian steps, indeed, play a very significant role.

(i) ***Preparation:*** This is the initial Herbartian step in which the teacher tries to explore the pupils form the standpoint of previous experience. He puts some preparatory type of questions which enable to awaken the apperceptive masses of pupils. Herbart advises to make this step concrete, short and to the point, pin-pointed, precise and effective. This is, indeed, a step to put the learner in an appropriate mood of reception by means of handing his previous knowledge and experience. To be equipped with the previous knowledge and experience is to be equipped with a new light to master new ideas. Hence, its importance as an initial and vital step in the method of teaching.

The process of preparation is one that necessitates recalling the attention of pupils by means of exercise of their memories or past ideas and experiences. It is, therefore, the duty of the teacher to bring the apperceptive masses of pupils to light. Then they will become conscious of and interested in new materials or learning items.

(ii) ***Presentation:*** This is a step for presenting new materials to the pupils by means of arranging and placing them psychologically. The objective of this step is to present new materials to facilitate pupils to apprehend them clearly and completely. It is also a step that ensures systematic and disciplined development of new knowledge. Its success almost entirely depends on how the teacher had dealt with the previous knowledge of pupils in the earlier preparation step. What is very much desirable in case of presentation is that the teacher should have the ability to ascertain and assess his own role, since continuous presentation may affect desirable and effective co-operation of pupils. Herbart insists on presentation of any idea in concrete form. This is all the more necessary in the moral sphere where experience, as he strongly advocates must begin with the most understandable and simplest situation. The main purpose of this step is, therefore, to make learning clear, concrete and vivid. The process to be followed by the teacher is to begin with the most easily understood, easily accessible and the simplest matters and then deal with the more difficult or complex ones.

(iii) ***Association:*** This step involves assimilation of new ideas. This takes place when a learner apperceives the new ideas by means of the old ones. New ideas are brought into association with the old and assimilated. A welding process so to say, it is a very important mental step that accelerates exercise of the logic of induction. As the new material is compared with the familiar or the old one, and significant points of similarities and differences are noted by the teacher, the pupil gets an opportunity to incorporate new learning material in his own mental furniture.

As this is a mental step, it is ordinarily omitted in the preparation of lesson notes by the teacher for practical purposes.

(iv) ***Generalization:*** It is a step that follows the step of association. The facts developed are systematically framed into a general statement or rule or principle. This necessitates reflection. The pupils are led to the concept of a general truth. It is a step that raises learning to the level of concept-formation. Herbart, therefore, believes that learning should be lifted to this level from the low level of the concrete and the perceptive. It is a developmental step — a step that lifts the mind to its highest capacity.

(v) ***Application:*** This is the final step where the child exercises his new knowledge to fresh and varied situations. By application of new learning materials, he testifies his own knowledge, its accuracy and marches on for newer avenues of knowledge and experience. This is a very vital step in the education of the child. The main purpose of this step is to translate the truth in reality that every idea must be an indispensable part of the functional mind and it must contribute to the assessment and interpretation of the child in his own unique, clear, and specific manner. The new knowledge acts like a tool for assimilation of new material. It is a test for the child in assessing his thorough and effective learning.

The Herbartians have made teaching a rigid formula and a formal process without any warmth and vitality — a fact which Herbart himself would never have approved. Flexibility of the steps is neither allowed nor encouraged. As a result, the Herbartians have done little justice to magnify the mind.

Again, what about the child's training of the hands? Herbart remains not only silent but also indifferent to the child's many-sided personality.

Herbart also fails to do justice to the inner man. He does not prescribe anything to catch a glimpse of the inner world of the child — a world that is too complex and far beyond the normal sphere of intelligence for his and his followers to deal with in the mechanical five-step method of teaching.

To conclude, it cannot but be acknowledged that Herbart has introduced for the first time a new methodology of teaching that is both scientific and mathematical, and teachers have been amply benefitted with his five steps of teaching. He has done away with the faculty psychology and given education a new meaning and significance. His scientific theory of pedagogy is still relevant and with certain necessary modifications serves as the most potent force in the education of the child:

> Herbart had in view the education of the youth in his adolescent years, when his mind and character are reaching maturity. At this period the intellectual life is undergoing its most rapid growth. While there is a vast amount of emotionalism, there can be no question that, for the higher moral life as well as for the intellectual, emphasis must be played upon grafting onto his nature as many interests as possible. Ideation, or thought, and will cannot be separated. The higher will is an informed will. Impulse and desire, however, do not spring from ideas, as Herbart imagined, but they cannot become will, in any high sense, without the assistance of ideas. Herbart was right when he endeavoured to form the circle of thought as the surest means of forming character. Ethical personality is, after all, not the product of biological, but of social evolution. It has not come from the struggle with nature, but has been wrought in the crucible of interaction with other humans. The processes of idealization and of self-consciousness have assisted in developing insight and moral ideals. Viewed from this angle, no theory of pedagogy has yet risen to compete with that of Herbart on the secondary and higher levels.
>
> — Frederick Eby : *The Development of Modern Education,* Prentice-Hall of India Private Limited, New Delhi, 1964, p. 495.

The five-step principle of education as suggested by Herbert is, therefore, even now a pointer to the way we think. Who ignores that our ideas and conclusions should be rigorously analysed and examined ? Who, again, denies the importance of testing and formulating newer ideas and experiences in a specific, concrete, analytic and scientific way ? What, of course, is nagging and mechanical is to consider every item of class activity in terms of lesson notes covering every step, but that also becomes lively and interesting provided the teacher takes worthwhile initiative towards negotiating this end-in-view. As teachers, are we really interested in making every lesson interesting, stimulating, meaningful and living in and outside the class-room ?

REFERENCES

Boyd, W. : *The History of Western Education,* A. and C. Black, London, 1964.

Curtis, S.J. & Boulwood M.E.A: *A Short History of Educational Ideas,* University Tutorial Press, London, 1965.

Eby, Frederick : *The Development of Modern Education,* Prentice-Hall of India Private Limited, New Delhi, 1964.

Frost, S.E. : *Historical and Philosophical Foundations of Western Education,* Charles E. Merrill Publishing Company, Columbia, Ohib, 1966.

Good, H.G. : *A History of Western Education,* Macmillan, London, 1966.

Meyer, Adolphe E. : *An Educational History of the Western World,* McGraw-Hill Book Company, New York, 1972.

Morrish, Ivor : *Education Since 1800,* George Allen & Unwin Limited, London, 1970.

Power, Edward J. : *Evolution of Educational Doctrine : Major Educational Theorists of The Western World,* Appleton-Century-Crofts, New York. 1969.

Rusk, R.R. : *The Doctrines of the Great Educators,* Macmillan, London, 1965.

5

FROEBEL :
Education By Organismic Evolution

A front-rank educational reformer, most exalted and most revered on the one hand and least understood, censured as 'an eccentric old fool', mystic, atheist, dangerous revolutionist and symbolist on the other, Froebel believes that education leads a child to understand and appreciate the law of Divine Unity within itself. According to him, the universe is nothing but a unity, one and a whole. The purpose of education, as he asserts, is to lead a child to grow up as a thinking being, both intelligent and self-conscious and the main purpose of teaching is to enable him to represent freely and consciously his inner law of Divine Unity by learning the ways and means thereto. As the most influential, comprehensive and stimulating educational reformer of the nineteenth century, he first formulates and practises his unparalleled principle of education that all education must be directed towards the free and spontaneous unfolding of the child's inner nature. As such, it must pave avenue of understanding and efflorescence on the part of a child of his 'relationship with the whole and his involvement in the totality that is God'. Today, Froebel is remembered as the founder of the Kindergarten. But the fact that he is more than that and holds a very significant position as a pioneer in the philososphy of education necessitates judicious evaluation right now.

Born on April 21, 1782 in Oberweisbach, Thuringia, Southern Germany, Friedrich Wilhelm August Froebel, deemed hopeless, headstrong and stupid by his parents, loses his mother in infancy and his father, an orthodox pastor, sends him to a girls' school. As a lonely, frustrated and neglected boy, he has a reading problem and finds his real partner and teacher in education in Nature. He is in deep love with everything associated with the world of Nature. Throughout his long country walks he makes friendship with the flora and fauna of Nature — plants, insects, stones, trees, lakes, rivers, ponds etc. All these objects of Nature have abundantly contributed to his concept of education.

Deprived of parental love and affection, Froebel becomes moody and subjective. He has no playmates and so his sensitive heart makes endearing kinship with hills, flowers, clouds, trees and other objects of Nature. At fifteen, he proves a failure in learning forestry and surveying. After a brief spell at Jena in association with Goethe, where he also proves a failure as he runs in debt, he switches over from a clerk to a manager of a country estate in vain. In 1805, he goes to Frankfurt to study architecture but, instead, he becomes a school master in a Pestalozzian school where he finds imperfection in the method of instruction :

> He not only disputed parts of Pestalozzi's pedagogy, but even then his mind's eye was catching flashes of a strange, uncharted land in the continent of learning. It was inhabited by little children — a place where they might unfold naturally and without grief, amidst affection and understanding, without the bedevilment of drill and duress, but in the gayety of song and play. Such was Froebel's vision of Kindergarten.
>
> — Adolphe E. Meyer : *An Educational History of the Western World,* McGraw-Hill Book Company, New York, 1965, p. 374.

In 1812, Froebel's desire to study minerology also proves a failure. In the war against Napoleon he serves as a soldier. In 1816, he opens a school of his own in Keilhau, names it the Universal German Institute of Education, offers, besides Pestalozzian pattern of education, nourishment through music and play aplenty but faces the charge that it is against God. Finally, he comes back to Thuringia, his native place, to start a school for children primarily named as *Kleinkinderbeschaftingungsanstalt,* later on renamed and shortened to Kindergarten. Meanwhile, his famous book *The Education of Man* is published in 1826. Later on he has also written songs and incorporates this in his book *Mother and Play Songs.* Though the initial endeavour at Kindergarten has failed, Froebel, the impractical educationist and philosopher, starts another institution of the same kind at Bad Liebenstein where with the kind assistance of Baroness Bertha Von Bulow-Wendhausen, the Kindergarten has acclaimed global glory.

Learning by doing, as Froebel thinks, is more strengthening, cultivating and developing than by verbal communication of ideas. He, therefore, stresses on self-activity in education. The purpose of education, as he advocates, is to unfold the inherent personality of the child and, as such, it must cater to self-development by means of self-activity. He makes a significant departure from Rousseau as an educator on the point that while the latter emphasizes on devotion to nature and development of an independent personality, he wants to maintain a certain cohesion between the individual and the society by means of education. So what Froebel wants to arrive at through education of the child is to bring about a synchronization between his inner harmony and those of the family, the school and the society. Thus his Kindergarten represents a miniature state wherein children enjoy freedom of movement and creativity in association with their little comrades. In the words of Professor Eby,

> Froebel was the chief modern thinker to view education as an element in the process of cosmic evolution. For him education is not the passing on of the funded experience from one generation to the next, nor the development of certain capacities or powers, nor the adjustment of the individual to his environment. It is, rather, a process which includes all these and goes far beyond them. In his first important book, *The Education of Man* (1826), Froebel indicates that education is the process by which the individual develops self-conscious manhood, with all his powers fully and harmoniously functioning in relation to nature and society. Furthermore, it was the same process by which mankind as a whole originally rose above the animal level, and has continued to develop to his present condition. It comprehends both individual and universal evolution.
>
> — Frederick Eby : *The Development of Modern Education,* Prentice-Hall of India Private Limited, New Delhi, 1964, p. 502.

To lead and guide the child to clearness is, as Froebel advocates, the main purpose of education. This clearness is concerned with the child himself and in himself that should be at peace and unity with Nature and God respectively. As he states,

> The representation of the infinite in the finite, of the eternal in the temporal, of the celestial in the terrestrial, of the divine in and through man, in the life of man by the nursing of his originally divine nature, confronts us unmistakebly on every side as the only object, the only aim of all education, in all instruction and training.

— Friedrich Froebel : *The Education ofMan,* Tr. by W.N. Hailman, Appleton-Century-Crofts, New York. p. 16.

Froebel contends that the child is inherently good. This goodness in him is divine. It encompasses virtues of different types. According to him, virtues of the lower order are courage, industry, prudence etc. These are connected with the physical life of the child. But self-control, justice, simplicity, fraternal love which are social virtues and are closely related, for their development, to games in childhood are also to be nursed in education. What is vice is either a complete neglect of development of certain original virtues or distortion from them. All absence of development, as Froebel believes, is the faulty method of education that fails to appreciate this truth. As he explains,

> A suppressed of perverted good quality — a good tendency, only repressed, misunderstood, or misguided — lies originally at the bottom of every shortcoming in man. Hence the only and infallible remedy for counteracting any shortcoming and even wickedness is to find the originally good source, the originally good side of the human being that has been repressed, disturbed or misled into the shortcoming, and then to foster, build up, and properly guide the good side.
>
> — *Ibid.,* pp.121-122

Froebel discourages and eliminates imitation in the education and development of a child. Let the child be allowed to engage himself in living, spontaneous and continuous activity to satisfy the inner craving of his nature as revealed in play. Unlike Rousseau, Froebel does not believe in catastrophic changes in the child. He does not conform to the saltatory theory of Rousseau, as it does not approve continuity and unity and a uniform law that governs all forms of efflorescence in every human being. The different stages of human growth viz. infancy, childhood, boyhood etc. are all equally important, and so, each stage is significant for some central tendencies which indicate the aim of education for that very particular stage unique in itself and depending on the preceding one. In the words of Froebel,

> The vigorous and complete development and cultivation of each successive stage depends on the vigorous, complete and characteristic

> development of each and all preceding stages of life .... the boy has not become a boy, nor has the youth become a youth, by reaching a certain age, but only by having lived through childhood, and further on, through boyhood, true to the requirements of his minds, his feelings and his body.
>
> —*Ibid*, pp. 28-29

Froebel believes that the primary task of a teacher is to make the child self-conscious. A creative and transcendental inner urge of the child necessitates proper development. The driving force within the child is to merge with his spiritual being that makes his union with God. As such, Froebel's theory of evolution is not mechanistic but spiritual, not utilitarian but aesthetic, not pragmatic and naturalistic but creative and transcendental. In elucidating the creative nature of man, he looks upon the life and genius of man as realization of self-expression as the 'inherited' promptings of his divine essence:

> Each thought of God is a work, a deed, a product, and each thought of God continues to work with creative power in endless productive activity to all eternity * * * * the Spirit of God hovered over Chaos, and moved it; and stones and plants, beasts and man took form and separate being and life. *God created man in his own image; therefore, man should create and bring forth like God.* His Spirit, the spirit of man, should hover over the shapeless, and move it that it may take shape and form, a distinct being and life of its own. This is the high meaning, the deep significance, and great purpose of work and industry, of productive and creative activity. We become truly godlike in diligence and industry, in working and doing, which are accompanied by the clear perception or even by the vaguest feeling that thereby we represent the inner in the outer; that we give body to spirit, and form to thought; that we render visible to invisible; that we impart an outward, finite, transient being to life in the spirit.
>
> —*Ibid,* pp. 30-31

Froebel asserts that the child learns through activities. Learning by and through doing is all that is inherent in the child, that deserves unfolding through exercise in active life. How should one be true to oneself unless one makes an exercise within oneself an active life? Froebel, therefore, suggests not to consider play a frivolous thing in a child's life but it has a profound significance so far as his self-expression and self-development are concerned. Just as a flower unfolds itself from the bud, so the child manifests himself in the joy of play, which is the soul of all activities. The study of Nature as Froebel suggests in his system of Kindergarten is important for the child because this is the only means to have a concept of God who is the source of creativity. He revolts against bookish education and emphasizes on country walks and activities like care of animals and gardening, games and music. All these allow the child to study Nature well, which not only make him socially and morally conscious, but also enlighten him from the religious and spiritual points of view.

Froebel's concept of Kindergarten heralds a new age in the history and philosophy of education. A garden for children as he indicates, it specially regards children as tender plants to be nursled, and educators and teachers play the role of gardeners. The latter provide for children appropriate and favourable situations through activities and materials for natural development. The primary concern of the Kindergarten is to enrich their perception and observation that effectively contribute to their understanding and appreciation.

Froebel harps on the play-element as the most characteristic feature of the Kindergarten. He thanks the creative energy of a child is best revealed through creative and spontaneous self-activity. Along with play he is in favour of intorducing pictures, songs and so on to boost the child's impression and expression.

Just as he stresses on allowing the child to memorize poems on Nature and life for development of language, so he considers the plays of the child, 'the future inner life of the man'. As he observes,

> Play is the highest phase of child development—of human development at this period; for it is self-active representation of the inner — representation of the inner from inner necessity and impulse. Play is the purest, most spiritual activity of man at this stage. * * * It gives joy, freedom, contentment, inner and outer rest, peace with the world. A child that plays thoroughly, with self-active determination, preserving until physical fatigue forbids, will surely be a thorough, determined man, capable of self-secrifice for the promotion of the welfare of himself and others. * * * The spontaneous play of the child discloses the future inner life of the man. The plays of childhood are the germinal leaves of all later life.
>
> —*Ibid,* pp. 54-55

Right from childhood, education should, as Froebel believes, be concerned with the development of sense perception. The mother draws the attention of the child towards the different parts of his body. This leads the child to understand the functions of every part of his body. He becomes aware of these activities and the growing interest in him activates him to know and appreciate more and more by means of exercising self-consciousness.

Froebel lays a great deal of emphasis on rhythm and drawing in the development of the child. Rhythm, as he believes, is the most important component to understand and appreciate art. If the child is allowed to understand and appreciate art through rhythm, it serves two-fold development within himself. First, rhythm ensures moral development in him. He acquires and exercises moral qualities like moderation and firmness. Secondly, he also develops and enriches self-consciousness by means of self-control.

As regards drawing, Froebel thinks that it is the surest means for the child to develop knowledge, exercise judgment and convey original and innovative ideas or concepts. Drawing also enables the child to identify different colours and think abstractly. This is nothing new for a child. Froebel believes that it is an innate faculty of the child as he is blessed with the innate faculty of speech. It also ensures his spiritual development. By means of drawing he discriminates between observation as such and inward vision.

Froebel primarily stresses on drawing for the education of the child because he thinks that it is the only means to give the child a sure entry to the inner world of symbols. Moreover, he thinks that through drawing the child will be able to understand any form of expression or language that stands midway between written symbols and things.

Froebel incorporates drawing in this principle and method of education of the child for other reasons as well. It sharpens the perception of objects. It also ensures the discriminating power of the child in observation and assimilation. As he clearly perceives, he develops the knowledge of number which is undeniably very essential to have an elementary but compulsory knowledge of mathematics.

Froebel believes that all education is a genetic process of activities and capabilities. How to develop an ideal atmosphere for the child to use the Kindergarten for creative activities ? Froebel introduces a series of building and other apparatus. These are properly graded from easier to harder ones. To be assured of the most perfect means for inner development of the child, he also introduces sand, clay, sawdust and the like. These materials serve as a parallel to the child's own world of creativity in the form of interest. What Froebel actually wants from introducing the Kindergarten as an effective system of education is to enable the child to enrich himself morally, mentally, physically, socially and spiritually.

The immense role of Froebel's theory of playway activity in education and the system of Kindergarten can hardly be denied. As Morrish reminds us,

> Rejecting as he did purely utilitarian considerations in education, Froebel saw some of the deeper principles of life enacted in forms of activity and play from the earliest ages on. The very game of life was to be viewed in the play of the child right at its inception.
>
> Play, in a sense, was a very serious business, and therefore had to be carefully planned to develop the right unities and principles for full being. Nothing was further from Froebel's mind than some of the free, unregulated play and activity sometimes seen in 'progressive' schools. Through play, educative play, regulated play, the individual developed a disciplined view of life, its complexities and responsibilities.
>
> Thus the Kindergarten was essentially a school for life, not the nursery playground which so many educators have seen in it. It was a place where the child could begin that natural unfolding of his essential being which was to go on throughout his entire life. It is not surprising, therefore, that Froebel saw the possibilities of an educational centre which would take in a whole range of schools from the nursery to the technical and the mothers' school. This latter he regarded as vital because of the child's tendency to imitate — a tendency which should be most carefully cultivated and with the best models and examples in mind. Hence mothers needed educating as well as their children. The gardeners (teachers and parents) had to be cultivated themselves before they could cultivate the plants (children) in their gardens.
>
> But a garden which involved harmony, unity and beauty was not something that could be allowed to develop in any haphazard sort of way. The best horticultural productions, in Froebel's view, were those which were planted with considerable thought and awareness of the structural and aesthetic content as well as of the methods to be employed to encourage growth and development. The child was a growing organism, and growth followed certain rules ; there was nothing arbitrary, for example, about his introduction of certain 'gifts' — they appeared in the child's natural development at certain specific and calculated intervals, as the child was assisted through

the progressive stages of his evolution.

> — Ivor Morrish: *Education Since 1800,* George Allen & Unwin Limited, London, 1970, pp. 202-203.

Why does Froebel give importance to the study of Nature in the education of the child ? This is primarily because Nature helps the child to develop his power of intuition. Himself a passionate lover of Nature, Froebel thinks that Nature is the revelation of God. As such, he believes that the child should be made aware of the hidden meaning of Nature in all objects that he encounters in and around himself.

Froebel maintains a regular programme of education for the child in direct contact with Nature. The weekly programmes of excursions into the valleys and mountains as he sponsors in his first Kindergarten at Keilhau are full of educational values. They enliven both the mind and the body. Children really find a refreshing atmosphere in Nature for their spontaneous and joyful activities.

To understand oneself in association with the understanding of other human beings is one of the most significant outcomes of Nature. Froebel, therefore, encounrages the child to study Nature in order to learn mathematics, physics, chemistry and other sciences. Nature unfolds man with all her objects and the child is christened to this truth to justify himself as a physical, mental and spiritual being.

Froebel's law of development of the child by means of education in the midst of nature also denotes his belief that man is nothing but a seed planted in a garden. As the seed unfolds, it justifies the creative force inherent in it. This evolutionary law of creativity should be translated into reality in the education of the child. At the backdrop of this evolutionary law Froebel harbours on a dynamic, self-conscious, progressive and spiritual philosophy of human development. As Frost spells out,

> To him (Froebel) the universe was a spiritual organism that creates itself in both the physical and the mental worlds. As he developed this concept, he came to believe that God creates himself through a dialectic that consists of action, reaction and equilibrium. This is dynamic, not static. God acts, and this action produces reaction, which finds a dynamic relationship in equilibrium, which sets the stage for further action, reaction, and equilibrium.
>
> In this process, self-conscious man eventually appears, a being able to understand the process and develop and education which will

further the process. Man is not the end of the process. He is a stage in the ever-continuing dialectic. Froebel believed in unlimited progress, 'Man', he said, is to be looked upon not as perfectly developed, not as fixed and stationary, but as steadily and progressively growing * * * It is unspeakably pernicious to look upon the development of humanity as stationary and complete.

Froebel was conscious of the fact that so many idealistic philosophies of oneness found themselves unable to solve the problem of evil. If the unity is good, how can it create evil ? His answer was that evil is not positive, but negative. If we analyse good and evil, we find that evil is a good that has been perverted in its unfolding. This perversion may result from neglect of the development process or from a distortion of the original goodness.

— S.E. Frost: *Historical and Philosophical Foundations of Western Education,* Charles E. Merrill Publishing Company, Columbus, Ohio, 1966, p. 371.

With the above perspective of human development, Froebel believes that the child manifests its inner nature in a psychological discipline. It is the duty of the teacher to lead the child in such a way through education that the latter may unfold the inner self in the midst of a stimulating and natural environment. Hence, the genesis and functions of the Kindergarten materials with a series of 'gifts' and 'occupation' suited to the development of the child.

The Froebelian 'gifts' and 'occupations' are very selected educative materials. These are meant for play and work by the child. These are helpful for every child to acquire certain definite ideas. These are introduced because they are valuable for imparting social, scientific and mathematical concepts in particular. The child becomes conscious of his inner self to respond to these diverse concepts as and when necessary.

In case of the Froebelian 'gifts', there are, first, six soft woollen balls representing six colours. With these six balls, the child gets, through playing with these, a clear and thrilling concept of six colours in course of distinction, comparison and contrast.

Second, cube, cylinder and wooden sphere are introduced as gifts. With these, the child, while playing, gets an idea of size, shape, hardness etc.

Third, a two-inch cube is divided into eight smaller cubes. These are given to the child as gift materials. With these, he learns the concept of a size and understands the points of difference between the part and the whole, the quarter and the half and so on. Moreover, he becomes interested in the defferent designs of construction.

Fourth, a two-inch cube is divided into eight oblong blocks (parallelopipeds). Another cube is divided into twenty-seven cubes. Still another cube is divided into smaller ones. All these are put in separate boxes according to their shapes and sizes. The applications of these objects along with wooden tablets, sticks of different lengths, rings of diverse dimensions and others amply contribute to having clear concepts in mathematics, arts and other subjects.

Froebel formulates his theory of transfer of learning in the form of symbols. Objects serve as symbols to the child and with this end-in-view he asserts that if the child is exposed to certain objects he will have an idea of their cosmic truths. The cosmic principles of unity, diversity and higher unity underlying these objects are as follows:

> The universe is a unity, one. This the child must be led to understand. How can the mother assist her child in developing this understanding? She can give her child several soft, coloured balls. The ball, round, with no edges or corners, complete in itself, is a symbol of unity. Within its name is the 'all', ball. As the infant plays with these balls, he will be experiencing a true symbol of God, of oneness. But he must also come to realize that wherever there is action, there is reaction; wherever he finds oneness, he also finds the many. One necessitates the other. Therefore, the child must have a symbol of diversity. That Froebel found in the cube, an object that is many-sided, many-edged, with many corners. This is given to the child as a toy, a toy carefully calculated to teach the idea of many, of diversity.
>
> To leave the child at this point would create confusion and frustration. He would come to understand oneness and diversity. Since Froebel's law of the universe is one of action, reaction, and equilibrium, he must give the child a third 'gift' that symbolizes equilibrium, a 'gift' that will lead him, through its symbolism, to an understanding that all seeming contradiction is cleared away in the synthesis of the opposites. This he found in the cylinder. Its roundness and its flat ends are taken from the ball and the cube and symbolize this synthesis.
>
> — *Ibid,* pp. 374-375

According to Froebel, flowers, words, any casual event and, indeed, every object of Nature represents an inner meaning and significance as a symbol. Why does he give importance to symbols ? Froebel has minutely observed that the child has a natural tendency for symbols, whenever he is absorbed in spontaneous activities. This is why Froebel considers symbolism an inseparable and indispensable part of the education of the child. Symbolization as a form of language or as the very genesis of mankind has also been emphasized by him.

> There can be no question whatever that Froebel correctly observed in the spontaneous activities of children a natural penchant for symbols. For this reason he considered symbolism a necessary function of the growing understanding, and felt that it betokens an active and creative mind. It is essential, not only for the activities of young children, but also for subsequent ripening of their ideas.
>
> Froebel believed that symbolization is a form of language. As the child has a natural afffinity for words, which are auditory and written symbols, so he has a spontaneous urge to create other symbols.
>
> Furthermore, it must be pointed out that, as a matter of fact, man has become what he is mainly through the use of symbols. Without them no progress above the brute would have been possible.
>
> — Frederick Eby: *The Development of Modern Education,* Prentice-Hall of India Private Limited, 1964, p. 527

Froebel's experiments with symbols to enable the child to learn unity in diversity and *vice versa* are undeniably important for development of certain concepts but they are subject to the following points of criticism:

(a) Froebel is correct when he states that words are symbols only for things but he is erroneous in the concept that objects or things carry within themselves the symbolism of their own;
(b) An object does not necessarily symbolize a single thing. It may, on the other hand, represent or symbolize different things;
(c) The efflorescence of symbolism entirly depends on the actual situation. It may vary from one situation to the other;
(d) The symbol of an object appears different to different persons, which may not be altogether wrong or ignored due to individual difference of approach; and
(e) Individual needs and experiences largely contribute to

understanding and appreciation of an object and the symbol it represents.

As regards Froebel's exposition on 'occupations', he differentiates these from 'gifts' by identifying as flexible materials. Weaving, painting, clay modelling wax or cork work with sticks etc. are some of the occupations which he has introduced in his Kindergarten. But the difference between gifts and occupations as Froebel makes, is not clear. He himself considers all acitvities as occupations and materials for these occupations as gifts. Now gifts as such come prior to occupations, and, in this regard, Froebel fails to provide us with clear and specific exposition.

What, then, are the principal contributions of Froebel as a pioneer in education? The following deserves reiteration:

(a) Self-activity is the key point of all real development;
(b) Creativity is the most significant area of development of the child in and through education;
(c) Constructive activity should go side by side with the creative endeavour of the child;
(d) Play should form an essential part of education;
(e) Activities and interests in case of the education of the child should be carefully handled to bring about significant physical, mental, moral and spritual development in every child;
(f) An ideal atmosphere of education in the home and in the family should be there for the child. As good education depends upon good women, the education of women should be seriously looked into for child development;
(g) The curricula should be in keeping with the different stages, of development of the child. These should be activity-oriented and geared to the purpose of individual and social development;
(h) Education is always dynamic and as such, the education of the child should conform to the fact that it is an evolutionary process of human development; and
(i) Education should cater to the qualities of self-discipline, self-dependence and spontaneity.

Froebelianism, however, suffers from the following limitations:

(a) Froebel's system of education has been slipped to mere method or creed. Formalism has eaten up the very objectives of education for which he introduces different strategies for child development;

(b) While Froebel strives for education of the child for individual and social development, he fails to maintain a nexus between the actual and the ideal, between the individual and the group;

(c) Froebel's introduction of play-way activities is rather dull as it makes drill compulsory. Too much control in play-mars individual freedom. That is why, children often show lack of interest in paly-way activities; and

(d) Froebel is not strictly psychological in his approach to education of the child as he fails to make a detailed analysis of intellectual development.

As Morrish points out,

> Froebel, though not a professional psychologist, saw the necessity of understanding as completely as possible the psychological development of the child as he grew into boyhood and eventually adulthood. Whilst he accepted certain broad stages of development— infancy, childhood, boyhood and youth — Froebel made no detailed analysis, such as that of the Piagetian school, of the intellectual development of the child. The unfolding of the essence of the child's nature was seen by Froebel more in philosophical than in purely psychological terms. But in so far as his educational theory has a psychological basis, it is a psychology of activism : man unfolds himself by continuous participation, by doing, by creativity. Learning was always regarded by Froebel as secondary to doing; in fact, learning should not (and truc learning could not) occur in vacuo.
>
> — Ivor Morrish: *Education Since 1800,* George Allen & Unwin Limited, London, 1970, pp. 204-205.

(e) A certain disrespect for learning is revealed in Froebel's under rating of knowledge;

(f) Froebel's philosophical approach to education lacks clarity on certian points;

(g) Froebel's law of evolution does not properly direct in the evolution of child life; and

(h) In introducing 'gifts' and 'occupations', Froebel unusually overemphasizes mathematical and other concepts without caring for the standard and the quality to be achieved.

With all merits and demerits of his theory and practice in education, it is undeniable that the promise with which Froebel has introduced the Kindergarten has abundantly flourished today. As a pioneer *par excellence* in education, he will always be adored and admired.

REFERENCES

Eby, Frederick : *The Development of Modern Education,* Prentice-Hall of India Private Ltd., New Delhi, 1964.

Froebel, F.W.A. : *The Education of Man,* Tr. by W.N. Hailman, Appleton-Century-Crofts, New York.

Frost, S.E. : *Historical and Philosophical Foundations of Western Education,* Charles E.Merrill Publishing Company, Columbus, Ohio, 1966.

Meyer, Adolphe E. : *An Educational History of the Western World,* Mc Graw-Hill Book Company, New York, 1965.

Morrish, Ivor : *Education Since 1800,* Grorge Allen & Unwin Limited, London, 1970.

6

MONTESSORI : Auto-Education

Education is not a process from outside but within. It begins with the child itself. It is never passive but always active. To be so, education at its centre must place the child. With the child as the centre of educational system for a definite psychological breakthrough which is termed as paido-centricism, Montessori brings forth a radical revolution in education of the child. She leads us to this present century by introducing a few major changes in the system of education. The traditional system of class-teaching has been replaced by *auto-education.* This type of education is fundamentally based on the principle of liberty. The child is allowed to enjoy freedom of atmosphere in learning, development of individuality and spontaneous efflorescence of personality. While in the traditional system of teaching, the curriculum and the syllabus are the same for one and all, in that of Montessori these are different for different children in keeping with the psychological theory of individual differences. She also replaces the educational system of instruction based on the wrong principle that children progress at the same road in all subjects in the school. Again, the emphasis so long given in the education of the child is not on the child but on the teacher. As a result, the child is relegated to the background. Montessori brings forth a radical change in this system by giving more importance to the child in education than to the teacher. She also considers the child more important than the subject-matter to be learnt.

Born in 1870, Maria Montessori a deeply religious Catholic is interested experimental psychology. The first woman to be honoured by the University of Rome with the degree of Doctor of Medicine, she has worked in a psychiatric clinic. Later on she takes the charge of a school for handicapped children. She is more interested in the environmental factors in education than in books and teachers. The appalling condition of the hapless children in Rome reeling under the dirt and squalor of the school buildings deeply touches her. She first declares the importance of having necessary standards of hygiene and health in the programme of education for children. Re-education should, as she thinks, be given more importance than re-conditioning or re-housing for children in any scheme of education. With these ends-in-view, she sets up her own school for children in 1907, which is christened as *Casa dei Bambini* or 'Children's House'.

Montessori's 'Children's House' actually tolls the 'knell of class-teaching'. So long the role of the teacher was not to educate but to instruct the child. His primary concern was to complete the syllabus of studies meant for children. The children fell a prey to mere informations continually delivered by him in the class-room. He found delight in burdening the mind of the little learners with the load of information. Very little attention or respetct was given to the child's own interest or attitude, appreciation or aptitude, knowledge or skill, understanding or critical thinking. No variation in progress was allowed to the child. In such an instruction-oriented education, the child was forced to be lost in the melee' of the group. Montessori urges a war against this type of formal education of the child by introducing the psychological method of education which incorporates the following:

(a) Education should be child-centric. It should give primary importance to the child's own way of thinking and learning by himself.
(b) The child himself is the most important factor in education. As such, the role of the teacher is to carefully and cautiously study each child from diverse dimensions of the latter's personality.
(c) Each child should be treated as an individual and unique in the sphere of education.
(d) In the education of the child, all instructions should be entirely based on the individual wills and aspirations, needs and interests, likings or dislikings.
(e) The child should be liberated from the heavy load of the syllabus. Accordingly, the child, and not the syllabus, is more important than books, teachers or the syllabus. No force should be applied in imparting instruction or guiding the child to learn. Let the child be allowed to exercise his own judgment in learning. let him be allowed to be his own guide.
(f) The child should be allowed to learn in a natural process.
(g) To be truly pedocentric, education should place the child at the centre of the curriculum and the time-table. Then, and then

alone, education will be a natural process which will come closer to the invaluable Aristotle's words: "The desire for knowledge is implanted in man : the mind grows as the body does — by taking proper nourishment, not by being stretched on the rack". Then, and then alone, education will, as Comenius poignantly asserts, "come to children as swimming to fish, flying to birds and running to animals."

(h) The teacher should not be an instructor but an educator. His main purpose is to observe the child in education and organize appropriate learning environment. He is not merely a teacher but a person of discrimination, a keen observer of pupils' activities, experienced, judicious in his concern for each individual pupil, sympathetic, discriminating and endowed with human sensibilities. In the words of Montessori, 'instead of falicity of speech she (the teacher) has to acquire the power of silence; instead of teaching she has to observe; instead of the proud dignity of one who claims to be infallible she assumes the gesture of humility.'

— Maria Montessori : *The Advanced Montessori Method,* Heinemann, London, Vol.I. p.128

In her Children's House or *Casa dei Bambini,* Montessori allows ample opportunities to develop in children the inherent qualities of the head and the heart in a better physical and social environment. The teacher who is actually the Directress is neither a passive force nor is she satisfied with her silent physical presence but she actively associates herself with children to boost their creativity and spontaneity. She is very keen in observing the different occupations of each and every child. She actually watches the role of children themselves as psychological observers. She also directs, if necessary, to maintain order and discipline and sets before him with every care and caution ways and means to promote his observation as judiciouslly as possible. In fact, Montessori's method of educating the child throws wide open numerous avenues of development in child psychology and experimental pedagogy.

Montessori considers education as a means to develop the child according to his desire for seeking guidance from his Directress. Suggestions or examples for him should, therefore, be given as and when considered necessary by him. The curriculum and time-table should be oriented in accordance with the diverse tendencies of the child from physical, mental, social and spiritual points of view. As Morrish adroitly explains,

> Montessori argued, as Rousseau had done, that education should be pedocentric. The child had to be central in all our considerations of curriculum and timetable. Moreover, the child had to be treated as a child and not as a little man: Rousseau, too, had said that 'Nature wants children to be children before they are men'. Education was the means whereby, and the framework in which, the child was helped to develop in a normal way and to enlarge his awareness of the external world. Both the system, or organization, and the teacher existed simply to help the child as and when he felt the need of such assistance : but such help was to be unobtrusive. The teacher was not strictly such; she was a 'directress', providing the right direction when the child called for guidance. The essential thing was for the individual to gain experience through spontaneous self-expression and activity, and for this the child needed the right environment and time — time fully to express itself and exhaust its enquiry.
>
> — Ivor Morrish : *Education Since 1800,* George Allen & Unwin Limited, London, 1970, p. 214

The basic theory of education for child development as initiated by Montessori is to liberate the child form dependence on others. Let the child be allowed liberty in thought and action. Let him be allowed to enjoy freedom in all his activities as an individual. Let him not be lost in the melee of the group. Montessori, therefore, suggests that education must be individual. The class as such should be treated as a unit of organization and not more than that. It is absolutely of no importance and is, therefore, dead so far as it is considered a unit of teaching.

Humanity in all its intellectual splendour is, as Montessori maintains, best revealed in the tender age just as the ray of the sun and the unfolding of a flower are best revealed at dawn and with the first unfolding of petals respectively. The child like the sun at dawn or like a flower with the first unfolding of petals be allowed to enjoy freedom in spontaneous self-activity. Not a frightening or suffocating atmosphere of the school, the class-room or the teacher but a living and joyous atmosphere of spontaneity is what Montessori advocates for fullness of growth and development of the child. In a traditional learning atmosphere in the school, rigorous discipline and imposition of arbitrary tasks tell, as she points out, heavily upon the spontaneous movements of the child and his inner development. To safeguard him from such rigour or discipline, the individuality in him should be adored and honoured.

Montessori defines discipline in terms of liberty which, again, is best manifested in activity. She advocates liberty for the total manifestation of the child. When she speaks of liberty or freedom for the child, she never admits absolute licence for him to do anything and everything as he wishes but ensures the fact that discipline achieved or enjoyed in course of freedom enables the child to a master of himself and regulate or control his action and conduct for his gradual unfoldment of the inner self like that of the petals of a flower from its bud.

The slogan for the development of the child with respect to discipline as Montessori proclaims is : Freedom first, freedom second and freedom last. She considers discipline a positive force that allows gradual development of the child in self-control, self-direction, self-dependence and self-activity in an ideal and natural atmosphere of spontaneity. To maintain it, no fixed time-table in the school is required, and absolute rigidity and fixed routine work are absolutely discouraged. Montessori categorically asserts that whatever discipline is maintained in the traditional school and its teachers is negative and, as such, fossilizes the child in a caged, closed and cornered class-room environment as an immobile and lifeless human being. She calls these hapless children in the class-rooms as 'rows of butterflies transfixed with a pin'.

Montessori, therefore, eliminates discipline for the sake of so-called discipline and for annihilation of the buoyant spirit of every child. As she observes: 'We do not know the consequences of suffocating a spontaneous action all the time when the child is just beginning to be active; perhaps we suffocate life itself. Humanity shows itself in all its intellectual splendour during this tender age, as the sun itself at dawn and the flower at the first unfolding of petals'. With rigorous discipline usually maintained in schools for children, every child finds himself in a gasping atmosphere of rules and rules that hardly allow efflorescence of intelligence or creativity.

Montessori considers the value of rest very important in the all round development of a child. This rest cannot be attained without natural action. Every act identified and performed in terms of rest from muscles to minds, shows how far it has been geared to perfection. Montessori allows rest or leisure as an opportunity for the child in education to seek better avenues of action than what has been selected or chosen earlier. Real rest, as she believes, is an indispensable part of 'the hidden' precepts of nature'. In her words,

> To act in accordance with the hidden principles of nature — that is rest, and in this special case, since man is meant to be an intelligent

> creature, the more intelligent his acts are the more he finds repose in them.
>
> — Maria Montessori: *The Montessori Method,* Anne E. George, Trans., Heiemann, London, p. 354

Why does Montessori give importance to rest as a component of discipline and why does she want to applly it in the education of the child? The answer lies in her psychological approach to the concept of rest. As rest is nothing but to seek out ways of acting suited to our nature, it is identical with play. The rigour of discipline can be eliminated by means of play. It serves as a balance between the work to be perform by the child and the child itself as a performer. It re-activates and acts like an emotional safety valve and leads one towards goodness.

Montessori considers discipline an avenue of inner fulfilment. This avenue must be joyous and processed through one's inner ordering of personality. This is not all. Montessori introduces such type of discipline for every child in education by means of work and play as would bring about a synchronization between the inner ordering of the child's personality and the order in the universe. It is, therefore, necessary that through discipline the child will be able to regulate his own behavioural design to make himself meaningful and worthy of his own personality. Self-discipline is the real road to be meaningful and worthy of oneself. Montessroi spells out :

> We do not consider an individual disciplined, only when he has been rendered as artificially silent as a mute and as immovable as a paralytic. He is an individual *annihilated,* not *disciplined.* We call an individual disciplined when he is master of himself, and can, therefore, regulate his own conduct when it shall be necessary to follow some rule of life.
>
> —*Ibid,* p.86

Freedom in activity for the child does not, as Montessori points out, mean nurturing indiscipline. The offending and annoying propensities of a child necessitates an efficient check. To be activily disciplined is to be aware of such limitations, and so the Directress in Montessori's Children's House is always alert in arresting children, "with their feet on the tables, or wish their fingers in their houses". Positive prohibition against indecencies, ill-bred or rough acts always plays a vital role in the practice of discipline. Children should also be made aware of group interest by means of exercise of discipline.

How should one deal with an indisciplined child ? Montessori's answer lies in handling the child's instinctive designs. The instincts are actually the rudimentary parts of a person's character. They force a person to act. What is very important in case of dealing with a child to be well-disciplined in action and contemplation is to carefully negotiate with his instincts. A bundle of instincts often crude and unexercised as a child is, he practically necessitates an endearing nursling of his good instincts and elimination of the bad ones for motivational forces in education. To channelize or sublimate the instincts of the child is the best way to combat indiscipline. So any attempt at thwarting the instincts which are the prime movers of his action may prove fatal.

Montessori is averse to class teaching, for it fails to pay proper attention to the child as an individual. Moreover, the relation between the child and the teacher cannot be close and intimate. As a consequence, the child cannot open out his difficulties to the teacher. Nor is the teacher in a position to locate the difficulties and deficiencies of every individual learner and do justice to each of them. In her own Children's House, the Directress pays enough attention to every child, diagnoses the limitations of freedom, self-discipline and every activity of the child at work and prescribes appropriate measures to eliminate the limitations and accelerate the positive qualities of self-enrichment, self-awareness and self-development. Montessori, however, fails to impress upon the positive aspects of class-teaching that eliminate emotional imbalance through group instruction, better motivation and more purposeful socialization. She ignores that a balance between individual and group instruction is what is needed for an ideal strategy for guiding and supervising the child towards his all round development of personality.

Montessori emphasizes on the application of the scientific methods of observation and experiment in education. The importance of sense-training as she advocates opens a new chapter in the education of the child. In fact, she introduces in her Children's House the training of the senses very judiciously. She suggests isolation of the senses whenever necessary for identification and assimilation of each of the senses in relation to objects. Actually perceptual training, the training of senses cannot ignore the value of transfer. Again, the value of the powers of an individual sense does not entirely depend on itself alone but in association with others. But enrichment of every sense organ as Montessori suggests in her method of education is undeniable. As Morrish elucidates,

> Children had to be trained to look after themselves and to be essentially independent of others, whilst at the same time able to combine with others when the situation demanded it. In the training of the senses Montessori believed that one should isolate them whenever it was possible. If children were being trained for acuity of hearing then visual perception was minimized and the exercises were applied in both darkness and silence; similarly, the development of the tactile sense was accomplished by blind folding the subjects and presenting only tactual stimuli. These were methods which Montessori had applied to the handicapped and deficient, and she argued that they could equally work for normal subjects. In her development of this theme she found that she could devise particular objects and materials (just as Froebel devised certain 'gifts') which would assist in sense-discrimination. Such as perception of form, and size and weight, acuity of hearing, sight and touch, and a nice discrimination of colour. Coupled with this realistic, practical sensory training was mental training in association, recognition of objects, and recall of names corresponding with objects.
>
> — Ivor Morrish: *Education Since 1800,* George Allen & Unwin Limited, London, 1970, p.215.

It is interesting to note in this connection that as an Assistant Doctor at the Psychiaric Clinic of the University of Rome, Montessori takes up her assignment of educating children with mental and physical deficiencies. She has her experience of observing the method of treatment of the feeble-mined children in the asylum by Edouard Seguin, a French physician. But she does not like this method. Education, as she advocates, is more important than medical treatment. Accordingly, as a Directress of the Orthophrenic School in Rome in later years, she introduces the training of the senses through education for feeble-minded children. She emphasizes on the fact that education is nothing but an adjustment to the external world and, as such, the light of the external world can have a free access to the dark chamber of the mind through training of the senses. School discipline, too, entirely depends on how the child is guided towards exercise of his senses.

In her own school *Casa dei Bambini,* Montessori introduces free-activity of the child to have freedom in exercise of the senses. The school environment is so well adjusted to the exercise of freedom in learning that the child enjoys the fruits of creativity and spontaneity of his own in an ideal and practical setting:

> Free activity is the keynote of the Montessori score. One discerns it in the absense of the conventional classroom decor. In place of the familiar files of desks and benches in those days unalterably essential to the progress of learning, Montessori's *Casa dei Bambini* was served by common place chairs and tables, dwarf-sized to accommodate their users, who if the mood assailed them, were free to haul them about to any spot that suited them. Every Montessori chamber was enriched by the presence of basins, soap, soap dishes, and similar aids to sanitary welfare, in order to promote what Montessori called 'exercises in practical life'. Based on the idea that freedom implies self-sufficiency, these exercises sought to train the growing young to master such essential knacks and know-hows as dressing, maintaining themselves clean and tidy, dusting and sweeping, table-setting, meal-serving and the like. Even the youngest in Montessori's infantry were put upon perfecting themselves in lacing and buttoning, whose mastery in days before the present zipper millenium, was pre-requisite to a successful and happy life, but which, it is easy to forget, represented a formidable trail to young and unpractised fingers.
>
> — Adolphe E. Meyer : *An Educational History of the Western World,* McGraw-Hill Book Company, New York, 1972, p. 469.

Montessori aims at free activity not at the cost of good manners, social order and harmony, nor even at the misuse of freedom to be identical with licence. In her own Children's House where children aged three to seven play and work under the supervision of a Directress who does not act as a passive onlooker but as an active observer. Let there be no intervention or discouragement but fillip and hope which should form the essential qualities of the teacher as a Directress and guide. She, therefore, advocates maintenance of records of all activities by the child as a learner, and like a watchful mother encourages him for his good behavioural manifestations and suggests guidelines for changing, moulding or modifying his bad or erroneous activities by means of healthy and fruitful alternatives. As 'a perpetual president in the Little Republic' as Nunn attributes to the teacher, her role is to guide the child to have keen eyes, cautious ears and careful hands that play their vital role in the education for fullness.

Arrangement of didactic materials and judicious manipulation of pupils' natural instincts are the two pillars of Montessori's success as a pioneering thinker in education. Her experiments on education are largely based on synchronization of these two aspects. The role of the teacher as she suggests is to study the child's free activities and exercise of liberty in a scientific manner. Both physically and mentally, each child should find out solutions to the problems arising out of the task already selected for performance by him and not dictated by his teacher or the Directress. The main purpose of such type of auto education is to allow the child to negotiate all difficulties in learning by means of exercise of his individual power of thinking and reasoning.

Montessori introduces different types of didactic apparatuses to facilitate training of the different sense organs of each child. These are specially prepared scientific and educational appliances suited to the various needs of sense training. The following appliances need special mention in this connection:

(i) Wooden balls
(ii) Beads and buttons
(iii) Rectangular tables
(iv) Wooden cylinders
(v) Closed boxes of different sizes and shapes
(vi) Musical bells
(vii) Pianos
(viii) Pyramids
(ix) Sand paper
(x) Wax
(xi) Dolls of different heights
(xii) Prisms
(xiii) Coloured rods and other articles
(xiv) Cards

The senses of sight, hearing and touch are three most essential and powerful factors of knowledge. Therefore, Montessori stresses on the perceptions of sight, hearing, feeling and touch and so on in the education of the child. The training of the eyes by means of presenting wooden cylinders, pyramids, table etc. of different perceptual dimensions allows the child to have accurate sense training in observation. Again, when he is supplied with articles of different sizes and shapes and directed or guided to arrange them systematically in a frame in accordance with their shapes and sizes, his training of perception of form finds an appropriate avenue of perception.

In case of training for the child's sense of hearing, Montessori prescribes pianos, musical bells and closed cylindrical boxes. He is allowed to hear and enjoy sounds coming out of these different articles and instruments and trained in the power of discrimination of sounds. He also learns the concepts of stillness of sound when all the instruments and appliances of sound come to a stop and silence reigns supreme.

The concepts of roughness and smoothness, thickness and thinness, height and weight are introduced by sand paper, wax, dolls, sticks etc. Here, again, the child develops the power of discrimination between what is smooth and what is rough, what is thick and what is thin, what is tall and what is short and the like. The exercise of discriminative power in each child is carefully noticed and evaluated by the teacher in terms of attitude, aptitude, interest and other psychological points of view.

With elaborate sensory exercises, Montessori thinks that every child will be able to discover new horizons of intellectual development along with developments in other dimensions — physical, social, cultural, aesthetic, moral, spiritual and so on. With the training of the senses, the Directress will be able to lead the little learner from concrete to abstract from direct to indirect ideas and will also enable the latter to be acquainted with the exercise of association of ideas.

Montessori's main purpose of training of the sense-organs for children is to bring about a radical change in learning environment. Children will be able to exercise their power of perception, discrimination, appreciation or interpretations of diverse sensations. These contribute a lot to mental development. Attention and interest are both nursled not forcefully but in a congenial atmosphere of creativity, freedom and spontaneity. As such, readiness to learn plays a significant part in the education of the child

Montessori makes a revolutionary change in the usual method of teaching writing. She thinks that the skill of writing should be taught earlier than the skill of reading. She considers writing easier than reading because it is almsot entirely a physiological training — training of the motor skill while reading is a complex activity that involves in the perfect unison of the senses of sight and sound. Morrish analyses the Montessorian approaches to reading and writing as follows:

> Montessori believed that in the more didactic processes writing ought to precede reading. This again was based largely on a psyiological approach which saw in writing the involvement of the child mainly in muscular activity. Reading, on the other hand, involved more than the muscular movement of the eyes, it required some interpretation of the signs presented to the eyes, which was a

mental activity, and the management of the voice. In writing Montessroi sought to provide facility and skill in letter production without involving the child's mind initially in meaning. To hold and manipulate a pen freely as an instrument was in itself a skill requiring considerable concentration and adaptability; and the formation of letters was reduced to a piece of sheer mechanism, or mechanical copying. The next stage was to produce writing which expressed ideas, and then finally writing from dictation through the analysis phonetically of the spoken word. Thus, when the child reached the stage of reading it was not a question simply of an effort to produce certain accurate sounds, but rather an immediate response to meaning, to the ideas within the context of the words read. Montessori was oposed to the sort of reading where the child may eventually read a sentence correctly, without hesitation, but still have no understanding of its meaning. Reading was already prepared for in the process of writing.

— Ivor Morrish: *Education Since 1800,* George Allen & Unwin Limited, London, 1970, p.216.

Montessori makes the art of writing and reading really interesting to the children. She is aware of training of their tactile, visual and dimensional sense organs necessary for coordination in learning how to write. In case of writing, she suggests the training and exercise of the following:

(i) The muscular mechanism necessary for holding and using the instrument in writing;
(ii) To fill in the outlines of a geometrical form on a paper;
(iii) Learning to know and write the alphabets by means of letters mounted on card-board. Exercises of visual-muscular image of the alphabets are thus made;
(iv) Introducing concepts of straight, vertical, horizontal, circular and curved lines through drawing. Demonstration of writing letters through exercise of visual memory by means of identification of the different shapes of letters; and
(v) Exercise of the composition of words through selection of cardboard letters from a set of boxes and mounting them on the board as directed or guided by the Directress.

In case of the method of teaching of reading, Montessori suggests the following strategies:

(i) Selection of a particular slip of paper or card upon which a letter, a word, or a phrase is clearly and legibly written;
(ii) Introducing different toys to the child;
(iii) Showing the particular letter, word or phrase to the child and directing him to find out or point the same letter, word or phrase to be found on the painted wall;
(iv) Showing the model or picture of a particular thing or object, animal or the like and directing the child to prove his power of recognition by means of identification of the same from the painted wall;
(v) Familiarization of sounds of words with objects or even with relevant pictures, models, charts etc.
(vi) Recognition of words arranged through letters, pictures etc.
(vii) Learning correct pronunciation of words through exercise of sound-patterns repeatedly and cautiously;
(viii) Dramatization of a particular story or event or picture or model or chart as the case may be and direct involvement of children therein. They themselves select scenes, costumes etc. out of their own initiative; and
(ix) Introducing recitation and songs appropriate for correct and refined reading habit.

Montessori's method of the development of the reading skill as above has, however, been subject to criticism. As Meyer observes,

> Despite the fact that her learners had demonstrated an ability to read with fluency, she, nevertheless, harbored some doubts. Did the words the youngster quarried from the printed page and minted into oral speech actually mean that he was master of the reading mystery? Did he, in truth, really fathom the message that spilled so freely from his lips? Or was his rendition a mere mechanical tour de force which made no more sense to him than the recital of so much syllabic mumbo-jumbo? Such and other questions the doctor never successfully answered. The one certainly she was able to muster was that in order to bring about proficiancy in reading, thc best assurance for success was an 'explosion' into composition. Let the novice burst into a piece of connected writing, however puerile, and he will, Montessori was convinced, invest his words with meaning and read what he has connected with understanding. Meanwhile, however, the doctor

had made up her mind that "it is unnatural for children under six, unless they are overstimulated, to read or write continuously".

— Adolphe E. Myer: *An Educational History of the Western World,* McGraw-Hill, Book Company, New York, 1972, p. 472.

Montessori eliminates fairy-tales and fantasies since these are mere compensations of repressed interests and harmful to normal development of the child. She ignores the appeal of such fairy tales and fantasies as would fruitfully contribute to the enrichment of the child's power of imagination. Her philosophy of education is also criticized from the following points of views:

(i) Montessori's method is primarily directed towards education of the feeble-minded children. Therefore, this method may not be suitable for normal children as they are habituated to have added, enriched and effective exposures from home, family and the society;

(ii) Her method seems to smack of faculty psychology. The errors of faculty psychology from her method of training of the sense organs of children necessitate a foolproof and objective clearance;

(iii) Pupil freedom in her method has been given excessive allowance. This goes against pedagogical justification;

(iv) There is a possibility of spoon-feeding in her method of educating the child as the latter is often mesmerized in the world of objects from their external appearance and hardly finds necessary scope for thinking alone and grasping the inherent meaning of things unseen, untouched, or even unheard;

(v) Her method of education for the child fails to assert the fact that it is erroneous to guide the child to learn in the arrangement of occupations without caring for the typical individual world of the child - his own occupations, tastes and temparaments even though ostensibly erroneous; and

(vi) Her theory of transfer of training goes against the principle that transfer is not possible without identical situations.

With all criticisms as above, it is undeniable that Montessori adds a new chapter in the modern history of education of the child by her incomparable contribution to auto-education:

In her philosophy of education Montessori produced a strange amalgum of idealism, naturalism and realism. Her idealism sprang from her acceptance of spiritual ideas and her religious, Catholic background. Her naturalism derived from the environmental situation of the children she dealt with Rome, and a recognition of their need to live a full, free, healthy life without the restrictive influences of generations of social decay and conditions which lacked even the elements of sanitation, cleanliness and hygiene. But truth and knowledge she felt could be reached only through immediate, physical, sensuous environmental 'realities', so that, whilst emphasizing the value of religion, morality, music, art and poetry she underlined also the vital importance of things and the child's relationship with them. Her philosophy was not so much consciously syncretic as unconsciously synthetic. There was, in all her thinking, a happy union of the ideal, the natural and the real.

— Ivor Morrish : *Education Since 1800,* George Allen & Unwin Limited, London, 1970, pp. 214-215.

How far do we materialize Montessori's philosophy of education in our modern pedagogy to make a happy unison of 'the ideal, the natural and the real' in our thinking ?

REFERENCES

Meyer, Adolphe E. : *An Educational History of the Western World,* McGraw-Hill Book Company, New York, 1972.

Montessori, Maria : *The Advanced Montessori Method,* Heineman, London.

Morrish, Ivor : *Education Since 1800,* George Allen & Unwin, London, 1970.

Rusk, R.R. : *Doctrines of the Great Educators,* Macmillan, London, 1965.

Standing, E.M. : *Maria Montessori: Her Life and Work,* Fresno, Academy Guild Press, London, 1962.

7

DEWEY : Progressive Education

Of all the educational thinkers and philosophers of the twentieth century, Dewey ranks the most prominent position. He is the forerunner of progressive education. He never accepts any principle of education wihtout having any relevance to life and society, without reasoning or scientific basis. As a celebrated educator, his influence is undeniably profound as he believes everything in terms of education and life. In the reform for relevance, his contribution to the arena of education is always a guiding force to all educational thinkers and philosophers in modern times.

Born on October 20, 1859 at Burlington, Vermon; U.S.A, John Dewey has received his early education in the local public school. Graduated in 1879 from the University of Vermont he has worked as a teacher in a country school for sometime and thereafter joins John Hopkins University, studies under G. Stanley Hall, Herbert B. Adams, and Charles S. Peirce, the renowned pragmatic philosopher of the day, and receives his Ph.D.degree in 1884. He has taught at the Universities of Michigan, Minnesota, Chicago and Columbia where he is honoured as Professor Emeritus after ten years of distinguished service as an educator. As a prolific thinker, philosopher, educationist and humanist he has amply contributed to the different disciplines — ethics, aesthetics, politics, history, philosophy and psychology upto the age of 92 till the end comes on June 1, 1952.

Sensing that the sterile educational system in his days can only be changed by means of bringing about a real learning situation through day-to-day human relationship, Dewey presents before us four specific problems. These are, as he thinks necessary, to be considered for a vibrant and sound educational system:

(1) What can be done, and how can it be done, to bring the school

into closer relation with the home and neighboured life—instead of having the school a place where the child comes solely to learn certain lessons? What can be done to break down the barriers which have unfortunately come to separate the school life from the rest of the everyday life of the child ? ....

(2) What can be done in the way of introducing subject-matter in history and science and art, that shall have a positive value and real significance in the child's own life ? .... Some statistics have been collected showing that 75 to 80 per cent of the first three years of a child in school are spent upon form — not the substance — of learning,the mastering of the symbols of reading, writing and arithmetic. There is not much positive nutriment in this ....

(3) How can instruction in these formal symbolic branches — the mastering of the ability to read, write and use figures intelligently — be carried on with everyday experience and occupation as their background and in definite relation to other studies of more inherent content, and be carried on in such a way that the child shall feel their necessity through their connection with subjects which appeal to him on their own account ?

(4) Individual attention. This is secured by small groupings — eight or ten in a class.

— John Dewey: *The School and Society*, University of Chicago Press, Chicago, pp. 116-119.

Dewey starts his experimentation on education for the child in 1896 in his University Laboratory School. His main purpose is to make the child aware of the new society. He introduces new methods and ideas that are suited to involve the child in a new environment for educational excellence. A group of about ten pupils ranging between 4 and 14 years of age is allowed to continue studies under the guidance of a specially trained teacher. The main thrust is to maintain a living class-room atmosphere where every child learns how to have the spirit of co-operation and sympathy as an ideal social being. Among other aims and objectives of this experimental University Laboratory School, Dewey reminds us of the following:

(i) to enable every child to learn weaving, sowing cooking and other daily activities;

(ii) to encourage all pupils to take part in practical activities;
(iii) to stimulate children in creative work;
(iv) to encourage children to exercise their manual skills;
(v) to foster in children the spirit of community feeling in course of sharing common interest, common pursuits and common aspirations;
(vi) to inculcate among pupils the spirit that the school is a community in embryo and second home; and
(vii) to enable pupils to share the natural development of their other activities leading to control, direction and leadership.

Dewey formulates a few philosophical principles what are closely related to his principles of education, of these the following deserve special mention:

(a) Knowledge is the by-production of action. By this, Dewey observes that in human development, it precedes action. Knowledge, learning or experience is a consequential factor of action. Action is primordial. Experience follows and modifies action. This modification takes place by repetition, redirection or inhibition. This is the innermost keypoint of learning;
(b) Man's mind is a very effective instrument or a tool. With its effective implementation, he raises himself above from other creatures. With this theory of the instrumental character of the mind, Dewey encompasses all aspects of the mind such as thinking, feeling, willing;
(c) All educational processes of the child should have their basis from the fundamental activities of home and social life; and
(d) As knowledge is, according to Dewey, always a social instrument, the social relations of knowledge necessitate nourishment in the education of the child.

An exponent of pragmatism in education, Dewey has learnt his lessons on pragmatism from two celebrated thinkers : Willliam James (1842-1910), a psychologist and philosopher, and C.S. Peirce (1839-1940), a logician and mathematician. While Dewey learns the coherence theory of truth as a lesson of pragmatism from James, he also learns the intellectual and analytical aspects contained in pragmatism from Peirce. 'An act or deed done or fit and right to be done', as the Greek word 'pragma' means, Dewey develops pragmatic method in education in his own vision of humanism.

Dewey may probably have undergone a hard intellectual experience from Charles Sanders Peirce but he has blazed new trials upon the principal thesis of pragmatism : change. The principal educational thoughts that have more or less influenced his educational philosophy can be mentioned as follows:

(a) In education, the child should be the focal point of interest. All education should be an active process that has a close relationship with the child's life and activities;

(b) In education, instruction should be a secondary factor in learning activities by the child. The main thrust in learning should be given towards problem solving. Techniques of learning how to learn are the essential outcomes of formal education where the scope of learning must be broadened;

(c) The pragmatic approach to education should assure that to guide and advise and not to direct is its progressive code;

(d) Education should form an indispensable and integral part of the process of living as opposed to education as a mere preparation for life. Education should be so geared as to enable children to be experienced in their time and place in the world;

(e) Education should be a democratic process. It should, therefore, allow an environment favourable for exercise of freedom; and

(f) Progressivism in education should eliminate competition and allow enough room for enrichment of co-operation. This will lead to self-improvement.

Dewey has sympathy for the optimistic views fo pragmatism but he is critical on rugged individualism. His own view on individualism rests on organisation of learning experiences. Thus a child organises his learning experiences in the school by organising the subject-matter through planned projects or social activities which are not necessarily detrimental to individuality. As he observes,

> A child's individuality cannot be found in what he does or in what he consciously likes at a given moment; it can be found only in the connected course of his actions.

— John Dewey : "Progressive Education and the Science of Education", Reprinted in R.D. Archambault, *John Dewey on Education: Selected Writings,* Random House, New York,

1964, p.176.

The above has been further accentuated when Dewey explains the individual factor in education from the point of view of restoring normalcy in his activity :

> Education must begin with a psychological insight into the child's capacities, interests, and habits. These powers, interests, and habits must be continually interpreted — we must know what they mean. They must be translated into terms of their social equivalents - into terms of what they are capable of in the way of social service. .....
>
> The child has his own instincts and tendencies, but we do not know what these mean until we can translate them into their social equivalents. We must be able to carry them as the inheritance of previous race activities. We must also be able to project them into the future to see what their outcome and end will be.
>
> — John Dewey: *My Pedagogical Creed,* Reprint, The Progressive Education Association, Washington, Quoted in Frederick Eby: *The Development of Modern Education*, Prentice-Hall of India Pvt. Ltd., New Delhi, 1964, p.619.

As a genesis of his pragmatism, Dewey does away with the distinction between ends and means. The 'end' for him is a collection of a series of acts, whereas the 'means' indicates the same series of activities regarded distributively. As such 'means' and 'ends' are equal.

Dewey's theory of truth is based on the fact that there is no such truth as absolute truth. In his relativist view, every truth leads us towards universal growth and evolution. As knowledge or truth, according to him, is never an end in itself but always a means or instrument to an end, his theory of truth based on Instrumentalism allows the role of the individual in reacting to 'truths' in terms of problem-solving from experiences. His reference to the whole or oneness broadens the scope of truth as an evolutionary process. His progressive vision of education has been appropriately summed up by Morrish as follows:

> Education was for him a realistic training in the breaking down of existing social barriers and in the developing of ever new links with the whole framework of society. The function of Education, if not

> its aim, was like that of an enquiry generally to act as a process of reconciliation of opposites, whether in the make-up of the individual or in that of the group, the community or the macro-society.
>
> — Ivor Morrish: *Education Since 1800,* George Allen & Unwin Limited, London, 1970, p.223.

The so-called progressive education as Dewey visualizes suffers from the essentials of eudcational process. It is not a contributing factor to insight specially into the science of education which highlights newer avenues of educational development, both in theory and in methodology. How far the learning condition is favourable to the child determines the essence of progressive education:

> In general, Dewey's rapport with progressive education was good - and progressives were confident Dewey was on their side - but he was, nevertheless, impatient with progressive education because he thought it was tardy in producing important additions and insights for the science of education and because it had not capitalized on its great opportunity to create an educational methodology which could deal squarely with the learning objectives of the new education. Although Dewey couched his rebuke in mild language, it is not easy to miss the generality of his meaning: progressive education was lagging on the essentials in the educational process - ends and means.
>
> — Edward J. Power: *Evolution of Educational Doctrine: Major Educational Theorists of the Western World,* Appleton-Century-Crofts, New York, 1969, p.347.

Dewey maintains a close relationship between philosophy and education. As such he difines philosophy as a general theory of education. In his own words,

> If a theory makes no difference in educational endeavour, it must be artificial. The educational point of view enables one to envisage the philosophic problems where they arise and thrive, where they are at home, and where acceptance or rejection makes a difference in practice * * * * if we are willing to conceive education as the process of forming fundamental dispositions, intellectual and emotional,

toward nature and fellow men, philosophy may even be defined as the general theory of education.

— John Dewey : *Democracy and Education,* The Macmillan Company, New York, 1955, p.411.

Every philosophy of education, as Dewey suggests, begins with the belief in man. He does not believe philosophy as the unifier or custodian of all knowledge, but regards it as a mirror of social life. The function of an educational philosopher is not to discover the inherent meaning of the universe for drawing conclusions from man and his relationship to the universe but to continually derive meaning out of the diverse avenues or components of human experience. As such, it should neither be concerned with metaphysical reality nor with whatever is abstract, but with the abilities and interests of mankind.

The processes of thinking as Dewey suggests through five logically distinct steps show how the philosophyof education in relation to thinking scientifically and progressively can be effectively cultivated. Indeed, the following processes as described by Dewey pave avenues for the recent methodologies in education viz., the activity method, the project method, the functional method and the problem method :

(1) The first stage is a state of confusion, doubt and perplexity owing to the fact that the individual is involved in an incomplete situation whose full nature and significance have not yet been ascertained. In terms of education, the pupil must have a problem, which should be his own.

(2) The second stage is an attempt at a conjecture, a tentative interpretation of the given data, attributing to them a tendency to produce certain consequences. In terms of the pupil, his problem must be a real one, that is, real to himself, and a stimulus to further thought.

(3) The third stage is a careful examination, exploration, survey and analysis of every available consideration that would help to clarify and define further the problem under consideration. Here the pupil must have the necessary information and make the observations required to deal with the problem.

(4) This stage is an elaboration of the hypothesis in order to make it more precise and more consistent as it begins to square with a wider range of available elements and data. Here the pupil is in the position of the researcher, developing his ideas and

seeking his own solution.

(5) Lastly, the hypothesis is tested; one takes a stand upon the projected hypothesis as an organized plan of action to be applied to the existing state of affairs. The pupil must be allowed to try out and test the validity of his own conclusions.

— Ivor Morrish : *Education Since 1800,* George Allen & Unwin Limited, London, 1970, p.228.

As an educational philosopher, Dewey is particularly interested in the ethical principles underlying education. The training of intelligence, as he strongly advocates, must have a direct involvement with the moral experience of living in the society. The teacher should guide the student to formulate a valid and decent ethical code for social living. The training of good sense and sensibilities both from the moral and the emotional points of view should play a significant part in the education of the child. What is, therefore, necessary is 'trained judgment' that replaces mere information and knowledge. Direct and concrete action replacing the indirect and abstract one makes the training of intelligence more viable towards sociability and moral values inculcated through education. As Dewey spells out his ethical principles underlying education,

> The difference between mere knowledge, or information, and judgment is that the former is simply held, not used; judgment is ideas directed with reference to the accomplishment of ends. Good judgment is a sense of respective or proportionate values. The one who has judgment is the one who has ability to size up a situation. He is the one who can grasp the scene or situation before him, ignoring what is irrelevant, or what for the time being is unimportant, and can seize upon the factors which demand attention, and grade them according to their respective claims. Mere knowledge of what the right is in the abstract, mere intentions of following the right in general, however praiseworthy in themselves, are never a substitute for this power of trained judgment. Action is always in the concrete. It is definite and individualized. Except, therefore, as it is backed and controlled by knowledge of the actual concrete factors in the situation demanding action, it must be relatively futile and waste.

— John Dewey : 'Ethical Principles Underlying Education', Reprinted in R.D. Archambault: *John Dewey on Education: Selected Writings,*

Random House, New York, 1964, p. 134.

According to Dewey, to find out the legitimate relationship between knowledge and morality is the most desirable function of the school as a moral and social agency. Such type of moral education as would bring forth essential behavioural change should be an integrated part of formal education where the individualistic approach is compulsory. Let there be no separation in the school between intellectual and moral training in education. Otherwise, it will indicate the school's failure to play its role as a society with its own life and values. The sordid role of the school as a moral and social agency does not avert Dewey's attention and sharp criticism:

> Moral education in school is practically hopeless when we set up the development of character as a supreme end, and at the same time treat the acquiring of knowledge and the development of understanding, which of necessity occupy the chief part of school time, as having nothing to do with character. On such a basis, moral education is inevitably reduced to some kind of cetechetical instruction, or lessons about morals. Lessons 'about morals' signify as matter of course lessons in what other people think about virtues and duties. It amounts to something only in the degree in which pupils happen to be already animated by a sympathetic and dignified regard for the sentiments of others. Without such a regard, it has no more influence on character than information about the mountains of Asia; with a servile regard, it increases dependence upon others and throws upon those in authority the responsibility for conduct. As a matter of fact, direct instruction in morals has been effective only in social groups where it was a part of the authoritative control of the many by the few. Not the teaching as such but the reinforcement of it by the whole regime of which it was an incident made it effective. To attempt to get similar results from lessons about morals in a democratic society is to rely upon sentimental magic.

— John Dewey : *Democracy and Education,* The Macmillan Company, New York, p. 411.

Dewey's educational philosophy has been broadly outlined in his book *My Pedagogic Creed* (1897) which has been further improved upon and developed in his subsequent masterpiece in modern educational philosophy, *Democracy and Education* (1916). While explaining and eliciting the meaning of education, he deals with the following in his two books:

(a) Education, a social process, allows the individual to be in close relationship with social consciousness;
(b) The process of education is always from the unconscious to the conscious levels of human relationship where freedom is exercised by every individual learner;
(c) With the actions and reactions of the individual learner, education stimulates social relationship. The learner explains his every action from the social point of view;
(d) Education, to be meaningful and effective, should have a psychological basis. It is the educator who should carefully deal with the individual's psychological structure in insight. This will ensure discipline and relevance in work;
(e) The education of the child should ensure translation of all his instincts, tendencies and capacities into social equivalents. All his endeavour in education should have a sound link with the social tradition of the past which will broadly outline future social actions and contemplatations;
(f) There should a sound basis of education of the individual in concrete terms. It should not be a mere preparation for life, which bears almost no meaning at all since it is rather theoretical, but should be a way of self-understanding and self-control for every individual learner;
(g) Education as a democratic understanding of the society should contribute to growth of pupil-experience in relationship with the society;
(h) As an outgrowth of existing circumstances, the aims of education should clearly mean what is to be done and why it is to be done. Aims, should, therefore function as pupil-experience;
(i) Every aim in education is experimental. It is, therefore, subject to change in terms of pupil-action; and
(j) All aims of education should cater to the intrinsic needs of the student and not to some pre-conceived, remote, out-of-the way accomplishment of responsibilities.

All the propositions based on Dewey's philosophy of education as above highlights the school responsible for proper social environment. In thinking and doing so, Dewey does not minimise or ignore the responsibilities of teachers but certainly he would not allow interference of the teachers as creators of the educational environment of pupils. What should be role of the school? What should be the function of the teacher? As Power spells out,

> If the aims of education are distilled out of the process of living, and according to Dewey they are, then the school's importance is enhanced, because to a large extent it is responsible for the environments where learning and living occur. Without a doubt, in Dewey's conception of education, the school wore a new face. What is the school ? In the first place, it is simply a form of community life; its chief role is to maintain an environment for high quality living by representing present life at its best. Contemporary community life is so complex that its full representation in the school environment is out of the question. Hence, there is need to simplify and consolidate the finest living experiences. Even these condensed versions of life when organized in the school's progoramme must be graded and accommodated to the maturity of students. Educational programmes should be grounded on the earlier experiences of home life, but they must also maintain a constant contact with home life in order to assure a continuity of student growth, on the one hand, and to illuminate the values of home life, on the other. When the school is understood to be a kind of community life, it becomes a better agent for moral formation, because it maintains the unity of living and moral training. Dewey was always confident that moral formation had better prospects in a school where moral training was sought through the channels of proper social relations.
>
> Dewey did not mean to disenfranchise teachers or relegate them to unimportant places in the school's environment. Yet, he would not commission a teacher to be the creator of a student's educational environment. Stimuli for learning and control over the conditions of learning should not come from the teacher but from the total social environment of the school, and the teacher's function is to select experiences to affect the child and to assist him in responding to these experiences.
>
> The conventional machinery of conducting schools - grading, promotion, and the like - should not cast such a long shadow over education. Each might have its place, but only insofar as each could reveal the student's fitness for social life. In this way, Dewey's creed was applied to the school itself.
>
> — Edward J. Power : *Evolution of Educational*

Doctrine: Major Educational Theorists of the Western World, Appleton-Century-Crofts, New York, 1969, pp. 361-362.

The school environment, according to Dewey, plays a major role in the education of the child, and, as such, it should be as simple as to provide an appropriate social context in a progressive manner. It would not only react but also contribute to an enlightened miniature society. It should rebuke social ills and highlight social achievement in such a manner as to march forward for a brighter future society. All education for the child should, therefore, be geared to future progress with appropriate mental exercise. The teacher will not transmit but communicate newer avenues in the world of knowledge and experience to the learner, and, in doing so, share and participate in pupil-activities to eliminate the difference between the learner and the teacher.

> In such shared activity, the teacher is a learner, and the learner is, without knowing it, a teacher - and upon the whole, the less consciousness there is, on either side, of either giving or receiving instruction, the better.
>
> — John Dewey : *Democracy and Education,* The Macmillan Company, New York, p. 188.

According to Dewey, there is no ultimate aim in education and, as such, the aim of education is to be found within the process itself. The immediate matter of interest and attention largely determines the goal. Dewey's own explanation in this connection serves as an ideal exposure on education :

> It has all the time an immediate end, and so far as activity is educative, it reaches that end — the direct transformation of the quality of experience. Infancy, youth, adult life, — all stand on the same educative level in the sense that what is really learned at any and every stage of experience constitute the value of that experience; and in the sense that it is the chief business of life at every point to make living thus contribute to an enrichment of its own perceptible meaning.
>
> — John Dewey : *Democracy and Education,* The Macmillan Company, New York, p. 89.

As a process of living, education is, as Dewey observes, a continued revision or reorganization of experience:

> The process of education is a continuous process of adjustment having as its aim at every stage an added capacity of grawth.
>
> —*Ibid*, p. 61.

As the educational aims are determined by the child's own being alone, they cannot but be approximate all the time. To fix an aim in education permanently is to restrict the functional purpose and stimulating experiences that always find an avenue of refinement and further growth in flexibility. With continual changes of experiences, the child orients and reorients himself with the complexities of environment. The process of education then becomes the process of living as the heart of education becomes buoyant with ever fresh activities and experiences.

Direct experience is, therefore, a major step in Dewey's process of education, and whatever learning takes place in case of a child is always a by-product of his actions. Learning by doing paves path to deriving the fruits of knowledge and thinking in every subject for study :

> The first approach to any subject in school, if thought to be aroused and not words acquired, should be as unscholastic as possible. To realize what an experience or empirical situation means, we have to call to mind the sort of situation that presents itself outside the school; the sort of occupations that interest and engage activity in ordinary life. And careful inspection of methods which are permanently successful in formal education, whether in arithmetic or learning to read, or studying geography, or learning physics or a foreign language, will reveal that they go back to the type of situation which causes reflection out of school in ordinary life. They give the pupil something to do, not something to learn; and the doing is of such a nature as to demand thinking, or the intentional noting of connections; learning actually results.
>
> —*Ibid,* p. 181

With regard to the curriculum, Dewey strongly objects to the subject-based curriculum and introduces the pedocentric approach that advocates subjects as simply the sum and substance of human activities. Let the child be allowed to learn a subject through making a summary of his own experiences. In his *The School and the Child,* Dewey categorically states that the child is the centre, and the end. The child alone is the starting point. His growth and development will determine the ideal to be followed in the functional curriculum. The subject-matter is always connected with the personal experience of the child. It is the duty of the teacher to organize appropriate situations for the child in learning and contexts of experience bearing all the time in mind the forewarning that all experiences have only a passing value and will change from time to time. Dewey also reminds us of the danger of the 'new education':

> ..... it regards the child's present powers and interests as something finally significant in themselves.
>
> — John Dewey: *The School and the Child,* Blackie, London, p. 29.

As Dewey believes in education as growth, universal growth, he disallows the existence of eternal values. Ready-made solutions are alien to his process of education and, as such, he also disallows subject divisions in the curriculum. Social living and activity by the child are the focal points of interest in introducing every subject taught in schools. For example, literature should be learnt in the context of the appropriate summary of social experiences, history in relation to the record of man's social life, science in connection with social living and all other subjects in alliance with intrinsic social values. The pupils's attitudes and interests will pave the avenue of learning these subjects and not according to the formalized patterns primarily dictated by the teacher with age-old theories and principles of knowledge, experience or learning. The subject-matter of education is never something complete in itself but, as Dewey categorically states, should,

> Consist of whatever is recognized as having a bearing upon the anticipated course of events, whether assisting or retarding it.
>
> — John Dewey : *Democracy and Education,* The Macmillan Company, New York, pp.153-154.

The curriculum is concerned with the real life situations of the nature of the child. Its content should always be ascertained from the diverse activities of the child. For this, Dewey emphasizes on the child rather than on the book, subject-matter or the teacher. The interests, inclinations, abilities and aptitudes of the child should be geared with a vocational thrust as well. As he considers the mind as a process of growth and not a fixed entity, he points out the stages of growth in learning through experience and doing in the three-fold stage of the school periods of life from the pyschological points of view :

(i) The period of play-way activities: This period ranges from 4 to 8 years of the child. A triangular relationship of home, the society and the child as a person be made in activities and habit formation;

(ii) The period of spontaneous attention: This period covers the children of the age group 8-12. Different forms of technical skill to secure for himself practical and intellectual control in every item of knowledge and experience are the learning items of the child at this period. A proper nourishment of his curiosity is the focal theme of education at this period, too; and

(iii) The period for exercise of the reflective power of attention: It is the outcome of a mastery over the different methods of activity, enquiry and thought and children undergo specialization for remote transfer of technical and intellectual aims.

Dewey's contribution as a pioneer in the philosophy of education is best understood in terms of future educational theories that have cropped up from his rich and varied role as an active educational humanist. As a matter of fact, all later educational theories and experiments are directly or indirectly associated with his liberal protest in education. As Max Wingo spells out,

> Dewey's educational philosophy was an organic element in his whole approach to philosophy. His basic educational views took shape along with his ideas in logic, psychology and ethics. Certainly the beliefs he held about educational matters cannot be considered simply as logical inferences from some predetermined ideas in logic, ethics or any other field of academic philosophy, though he found his studies in the various branches of philosophy to be fruitful sources for his ideas on education.
>
> The full impact of Dewey's educational philosophy can be sensed only by understanding how it relates to his interpretations of other philosophic questions. The philosophic tradition of pragmatism made important contributions to the progressive protest against essentialism and to Dewey's educational philosophy. The key ideas

on which Dewey based his educational philosophy have a larger significance outside of educational theory. These concepts are (1) the nature of experience ; (2) the significance of meaning and the pragmatic conception of truth; (3) logic as inquiry and its relation to scientific method, the nature of value, and the process of valuation; (4) the ontology of pragmatism.

— G.Max Wingo : *Philosophies of Education : An Introduction,* Sterling Publishers Private Limited, New Delhi, Indian Reprint Edition 1975, pp. 193-194.

Can the world ever avert Dewey's signal contribution to educational reconstruction ?

REFERENCES

Archambault, R.D. : *John Dewey on Education: Selected Writings,* Random House, New York, 1964.

Dewey, John : *The School and Society,* University of Chicago Press, Chicago.

Dewey, John : *Democracy and Education,* The Macmillan Company, New York, 1955.

Dewey, John : *The School and the Child,* Blackie, London.

Eby, Frederick : *The Development of Modern Education,* Prentice-Hall of India Private Limited, New Delhi, 1964.

Morrish, Ivor : *Education Since 1800,* George Allen & Unwin Limited, London, 1970.

Power, Edward J. : *Evolution of Educational Doctrine : Major Educational Theorists of the Western World,* Appleton-Century-Crofts, New York, 1969.

Wingo, G. Max : *Philosophies of Education : An Introducation,* Sterling Publishers Private Limited, New Delhi, Indian Reprint Edition, 1975.

8

TAGORE : Education Through Freedom and Joy

Education is always a look within to find out the best of one's efflorescence. It is an askance of the inner self-continual Challenging, unending. How to negotiate this askance of the inner self within oneself through education? How to be justified to education in the true sense of the term? For Tagore the global educator *par excellence* education for its better nursling and efflorescence in oneself should be imparted in an atmosphere of freedom and joy. While exercise of freedom is the best means of emancipation of the inner self, joy paves avenues of sharing and exposing the aesthetic sensibilities like Truth, Goodness and beauty that mark the victory and ascent of man.

Born of an exceptionally enriched cultural and erudite family in Calcutta on May 08, 1861, Rabindranath Tagore shows his apathy for caged education cornered in the four walls of city class-room which he leaves to liberate his banished soul not once but more than thrice . His inner self pines for the joy and freedom in education so long mercilessly massacred in an artificial and lifeless atmosphere and his disturbed and painful school life — 'a torn out line of a verse' as he significantly remarks compels his to brand the so-called schools as centres for parrot's training. The world of delight in an atmosphere of freedom is as he points out, to be exposed-in education because man is born of delight and joy—*ananda*. His own words elucidate the point best:

> Our life gains what is called 'value' in those of its aspects which represent eternal humanity in knowledge, in sympathy, in deeds, in character and creative works. And from the beginning of our history we are seeking, often at the cost of everything else, the value of our life and not merely success; in other words, we are trying to realize

in ourselves the immortal man so that we may die but not perish. This is the meaning of the utterance in the Upanished: *"Tam vedyam purusham veda, yatha ma vo mrityuh parivyathah"* . . . "Realize the person so that thou mayst not suffer from death."

— Rabindranath Tagore: *The Religion of Man*, George Allen & Unwin, London, 1953, pp. 145-146.

A grand unison between the Person and the individual through continual crystallization of self in freedom and in a joyous atmosphere of creativity is the end-in-view of all education.

For a real evolution of man's consciousness, Tagore considers education through joy as a means of liberation of the individual from the separateness fondled in narrowness of vision. Human love finds its best efflorescence in the world of delight revealed through the wholeness of personality. As Tagore poignantly asserts,

> Of all the creatures man has reached that multicellular character in a perfect manner not only in his body but in his personality .For centuries his evolution has been the evolution of a consciousness that tries to be liberated from the bounds of individual separateness and to comprehened in its relationship a wholeness which may be named Man. This relationship which has been dimly instinctive is ever struggling to be fully aware of itself. Physical evolution sought for efficiency in a perfect communication with the physical world; the evolution of Man's consciousness sought for truth in a perfect harmony with the world of personality.
>
> However, whatever name our logic may give to the truth of human unity, the fact can never be ignored is that we have our greatest delight when we realize ourselves in others and this is the definition of love. This love gives us the testimony of the great whole which is the complete and final truth of man. It offers us the immense field where we can have our release from the sole monarchy of hunger, of the growling voice, snarling teeth and tearing claws from the dominance of the little material means, the source of cruel envy and ignoble deception where the largest wealth of the human soul has been produced through sympathy and co-operation, through disinterested pursuit of knowledge that recognizes no limit and is unafraid of all time-honoured *tabus*; through a strenuous cultivation of intelligence for service that knows no distinction of colour and

> clime. The spirit of love dwelling in the boundless realm of the surplus emancipates our consciousness from the illusory bond of the separateness of self; it is ever trying to spread its illumination in the human world.
>
> — Rabindranath Tagore: "The Creative Spirit", *The Religion of Man,* George Allen & Unwin, London, 1953, pp. 47-50.

The idea of the 'divine humanity' that has consciously worked in Tagore's mind has prompted him to exercise in disinterested service his spiritual self in his own school. The special charater of his school, 'a living temple' as he has described,is 'to build for my divinity'. Education should direct the learner to a complete life. In his own school he highlights this end-in-view:

> In such a place education necessarily becomes the preparation for a complete life of man which can only become possible by living that life, through knowledge and service, enjoyment and creative work. This necessity was my own, for I felt impelled to come back into a fullness of truth from my exile in a dream-world.
>
> — Rabindranath Tagore: "The Teacher", *The Religion of Man,* George Allen & Unwin, London, 1953, p.166

A living and pulsating communication with Nature in her joyous atmosphere is the first step of education for fullness. A living school always caters to this joyous atmosphere of learning. Therein lies the genesis and fulfilment of freedom. Freedom and joy are so closely interwoven in education that apart from these two, education becomes meaningless nonsense. The gateway of truth becomes wide open only when knowledge enlivens us to enjoy the fruit of freedom that enables to grow within to be prepared for a journey beyond of consciousness. The truth that pulsates within awaits an avenue of freedom and joy only to find fullness of the vision of the beyonding of man.

As an incomparable exponent of freedom and joy in education, Tagore feels, and disseminates the vision of education for fullness from his own personal experience of 'a banished soul' while in the so-called school of learning and points out the psychology of exercise of the senses in an energizing atmosphere of joy and freedom. To know and embrace the world through learning for living in a perfect relationship with freedom and joy of the education of being is the first lesson that every child should be provided with in a school for an appropriate exercise of the senses. Let the 'non-civilized' self within him find a genuine exposure to react in an atmosphere of freedom and joy. Let him be allowed to taste freedom and find out the essence of joy in the uninterrupted efflorescence of the self in all directions for fullness. As Tagore elucidates,

> Freedom in the mere sense of independence has no content, and therefore no meaning. Perfect freedom lies in a perfect harmony of relationship, which we realize in this world not through our response to it in knowing, but in being. Objects of knowledge maintain an infinite distance from us who are the knowers. For knowledge is not union. Therefore, the further world of freedom awaits us there where we reach truth, not through feeling it by our senses or knowing it by our reason, but through the union of perfect sympathy.
>
> Children with the freshness of their senses come directly to the intimacy of this world. This is the first great gift they have. They must accept it naked and simple and must never again lose their power of immediate communication with it. For our perfection we have to be vitally savage and mentally civilized; we should have the gift to be natural with nature and human with human society. My banished soul sitting in the civilized isolation of town-life cried within me for the enlargement of the horizon of its comprehension. I was like the torn-away line of a verse, always in a state of suspense, while the other line, with which it rhymed and which could give it fullness, was smudged by the mist away in some undecipherable distance. The inexpensive power to be happy, which, along with other children, I brought to this world, was being constantly worn away by friction with the brick-and-mortar arrangement of life, by monotonously mechanical habits and customary code of respectability.
>
> —*Ibid*, pp. 172-173

Education for freedom and joy is, as Tagore strongly advocates, education for creativity. Unless a child becomes aware of his creative sensibilities, education turns out to be a mechanical training of the mind and allows no room for improvization. A 'symphony of response between life and world' which ensures creativity in children should always have a very wide room for exposure in education. The school is nothing but a living embodiment to experience and exercise creativity in the light of freedom and joy. In elucidating the essential role of a school, Tagore characteristically observes:

> The primary object of an institution should not be merely to educate one's limbs and mind to be in efficient readiness for all emergencies, but to be in perfect tune in the symphony of response between life and world, to find the balance of their harmony which is wisdom. The first important lesson for children in such a place would be that of imporvization, the constant imposition of the ready-made having been banished from here. It is to give occasions to explore one's capacity through surprises of achievement. I must make it plain that this means a lesson not in simple life, but in creative life.
>
> — *Ibid,* pp. 178-179

The simple ingenuity of a child to enjoy freedom in the world of his creativity should, as Tagore poignantly feels and makes experimentations in his own school for children in Santiniketan, be allowed to have its spontaneity. Austerity, and not affluence, makes the atmosphere of learning as natural as it should be and the child nourishes his creativity in such a normal and natural atmosphere of joy and freedom. What, according to Tagore, is of primary importance in education is to exercise and enrich the power of sensitiveness inherent in everyone, which alone paves avenues of human development and all-round excellence. As he frankly states,

> I tried my best to develop in the children of my school the freshness of their feeling for Nature, a sensitiveness of soul in their relationship with their human surroundings, with the help of literature, festive ceremonials and also the religious teaching which enjoins us to come to the nearer presence of the world through the soul, thus to gain it more than can be measured — like gaining an instrument in truth by bringing out its music.
>
> — *Ibid.* p.180

To emancipate the child from the abstraction and dullness in education is what Tagore considers to be an important role of the teacher. Let the teacher ignite the child with his own living spirit of creativity and freedom. Let him show how to be natural with the joyous atmosphere of Nature and explore wider avenues of creative adventure. In order to be so, he must be in close communion with the 'living traffic' with knowledge and informatics and share with his pupils a close vision of looking into every aspect of learning with an endless sense of curiosity.

Tagore, therefore, believes that the real pursuit of truth as we sincerely desire can only be possible when the learner's mind is living and not dead, and the subjects to be learnt are not dead but 'living specimens' of life and love, well-groomed in an atmosphere of freedom and joy. The end-in-view of all education should as he categorically observes, be to enable every child to develop a creative personality and the role of the teacher should always be to show by his own living example, the living avenues of the quest for creativity in freedom and joy. In his invaluable words,

> A most important truth, which we are apt to forget, is that a teacher can never truly teach unless he is still learning himself. A lamp can never light another lamp unless it continues to burn its own flame. The teacher who has come to the end of his subject, who has no living traffic with his knowledge, but merely repeats his lessons to his students, can only load their minds; he cannot quicken them. Truth not only must inform but inspire. If the inspiration dies out, and the information only accumulates, then truth loses its infinity. The greater part of our learning in the schools has been wasted because, for most of our teachers, their subjects are like dead specimens of once living things, with which they have a learned acquaintance, but no communication of life and love.
>
> — Rabindranath Tagore: "An Eastern University", *Creative Unity,* Macmillan & Company Limited, London, 1962, pp.186-187.

Tagore further explains his educational vision of joy and freedom in terms of creative efflorescence as follows:

> The educational institution, therefore, which I have in mind has primarily for its object the constant pursuit of truth, from which the imparting of truth naturally follows. It must not be a dead cage in which living minds are fed with food artificially prepared. It should be an open house, in which students and teachers are at one. They must live their complete life together, dominated by a common aspiration for truth and a need of sharing all the delights of culture. In former days the great master craftsmen had students in their

> workshops where they co-operated in shaping things to perfection. That was the place where knowledge could become living — that knowledge which not only has its substance and law, but its atmosphere subtly informed by a creative personality. For intellectual knowledge also has its aspect of creative art, in which the man who explores truth expresses something which is human in him — his enthusiasm, his courage, his sacrifice, his honesty, and his skill. In merely academical teaching we find subjects, but not the man who pursues the subjects; therefore, the vital part of education remains incomplete.
>
> — *Ibid.*, pp. 187-188

Tagore feels in his heart of hearts the wailings of the creative mind lost in the mad rush for mere exercise of knowledge and information. The absence of freedom of the learner to manifest his individuality in an atmosphere of joy and creativity deeply aches him. In a meeting on educational reconstruction convened at the Overtoon Hall, Calcutta he expresses his resentment against peril of intellect and efflorescence of individuality bereft of the blessings of freedom and joy:

> Our ideas are strengthened when they have been allowed unhindered avenues for manifestation. * * * Knowledge and ideas accepted with one's own intrinsic evaluational approach that incorporates comparison, contrast and assimilation as tools invite an individual to be more living and more courageous to voice forth one's unique way of thinking than merely accepting thoughts without having any reaction whatsoever. Knowledge judged from the latter kills time and energy and the individual's rich soil of expression remains intellectually virgin, fruitless and drab. Who cares for the peril of intellect and individuality ?
>
> — Rabindranath Tagore: *Siksha-Samskar* ("Educational Reconstruction"), *Siksha,* Visva-Bharati, 1973, pp.34-35.
>
> (Translated by author)

A radical break-through in education for freedom and joy can, as Tagore advocates, be possible only when education through the Mother-tongue is sincerely dealt with and nursled. Mother-tongue, as he considers, is, as it were, the breast milk of the mother, which has no substitute and which, when debarred from education, makes the learner alienated and lifeless from the living world of freedom and joy. As he expresses his indebtedness to the mother-tongue categorically:

> From the very early childhood, my entry to the storehouse of the Bengali language was unbarred. Whatsoever meagre the components are there in that storehouse, it was sufficient for the maintainance and satisfaction of the mind of the child. The fasting mind has not to lose its breath and tread on by limping on the upward path of the foreign language. As there was no regular and serious head on collision between learning and understanding, I was not brought up in the hospital of the school.
>
> There are other reasons for gratitude as well. The fundamental aspect of education is the pursuit to express in words the thoughts and ideas of the mind. It is the symptom of the healthy mind to make the very synchronization of this give-and-take process inwardly and outwardly.. If the foreign language becomes the principal medium of cultivation of expression, it turns out as if like the habit of expression of ideas through the mask.
>
> — Rabindranath Tagore: *Sikshar Swangikaran* ("Making Education one's Own"), *Siksha,* Visva-Bharati, 1973, p. 242. (Translated by author)

To foster the spirit of joy and creativity, education should be saved from the tyranny of the foreign tongue specially in case of children who are taught or perhaps treated in 'the hospital of the school' as Tagore clearly observes. In his celebrated and poignant article *Ashramer Siksha* (The Education of the Ashrama), he refers to the element of curiosity, the most natural and living one, that alone contributes a lot to the education of the child for fullness:

> It is the absense of curiosity that indicates the passivity of the mind. Today the nations dominating over the world have exhibited their indomitable curiosity upon everything of this world. There is neither any country nor any time nor, again, any subject towards which their mind is not being thrust forward. This living power of mind on their part came out victorious throughout the world.

* * * The education of the Ashram is to live in fullness. One can ascend the highest peak of the first class in the examination even with a dead mind. We are regularly accustomed to this fact in our country. It is seen that the very good students of the college secure titles of honour but never secure the world. From the very beginning, I had the resolution that the boys of the Ashram would remain curious of having immediate relations all around. They will seek, examine and collect. Here teachers whose visions spread beyond the horizon of books would assemble.

— Rabindranath Tagore: *Ashramer Siksha* ("The Education of the Ashrama"), *Siksha,* Visva-Bharati, 1973, pp. 248-249. (Translation by author)

In his own experimentations on education for dissemination of freedom and joy in an atmosphere of living and creative education in his own school *Siksha-Satra* christened by him as "The Poet's School", Tagore makes the learner widely exposed to the living elements of Nature where he finds a free atmosphere of creative spontaneity.* A real regeneration of the inner world of the child through such an atmosphere of freedom and joy in education is all the more necessary than mere parrot's training by means of bookish education. Freedom of growth which is so vital to the ascent of man finds a natural atmosphere in his

---

* It is interesting to refer in this connection to the activities of children in Tagore's school, Siksha-Satra:

> Records are kept and reports and accounts are written up revised and corrected giving scope for literary training in its most interesting form. Geology becomes the fertility of the plot; chemistry the use of lime and manures of all kinds of spray and disinfectants; physics the use of tools, pumps, the study of water-lift and oil engines; entomology the control of plant pests (ants, caterpillars, beetles) and diseases (leaf curl, wilt, bacterial attacks); orinthology, the study of birds in their relation first to the garden plot and to the world in general.

There is no room in *Siksha-Satra* for Nature study as an sbstract subject, diversed from life and needs of life.

> In life the child has to face the mosquito mightily perhaps the bug, or flea, the bacterial of ptyphiod, of cholera, of small-pox as well as the forces of nature which attack his trees, his plants, and his livestock. Nature-study is thus transferred into the study of nature in relation to life and experiences of life.

— L.K. Elmhirst : *Rabindranath Tagore: Pioneer in Education,* John Murry, London, 1961, pp.73-74.

experiments on education of the child to whom as he considers, Nature lavishly allows to learn simplicity in joy and creativity. Then alone, education becomes meaningful. The adventure of learning should have its focal point on how to delve into the wonderland of joy and freedom that care for inner growth. Unless the child finds this avenue of inner growth, learning becomes dull and mechanical, passive and artificail. In spelling out the aim of his own school Siksha Satra, Tagore observes:

> The aim of *Siksha-Satra* is, through experience in dealing with the over-flowing abundance of childlife, its charm and simplicity, to provide the utmost liberty, within the surroundings that are filled with the creative possibilities with opportunites for the joy of play — the reaping of succession of novel experience, to give the child freedom of growth which the young tree demands for its tender shoot, that field for self-expression in which all young life finds both training and experience.
>
> — *The Visva-Bharati Bulletin,* Visva-Bharati, Santiniketan, No. 9, 1928.

The unison of education and pupil-experience that Tagore seeks in his aim of education in exercise of freedom and joy makes education truly creative and meaningful. Such education is not only an unending quest for fullness of personality but also an adventure into the world of Truth, Goodness and Beauty through creativity. For this, education should afford the mind a genuine freedom of sympathy. Such type of freedom enjoyed by children will allow them to exercise the vision of Truth. They will then be truly christened with the imagination for the world of human relationship which is far more important for them than to have a bare theoretical knowledge of geography.

To replace mere rules and methods of learning by allowing a free play of the subconscious self of each and every learner is what Tagore aims at in his educational philosophy. Let the learner find endless delight in self-discovery and self-revelation through self-creativity, let him be exposed to self-identity, self-analysis and self-evaluation and let him be in tune with all objects of Nature to make a harmonious relation with everything in and around him. Then, and then only, he will justify himself to his own intrinsic fullness of being.

Education, therefore, equips the learner with the 'indwelling light' of Truth which, as Tagore believes, is best revealed in joy and freedom. The harmony of Truth which exists between the learner and the world at large is the harmony of human consciousness as exposed in the exercise of joy and freedom. His own exposition in this connection is significant.

> We are born conscious of one truth, which is for us the background to our knowledge of all other truths. It is the truth about myself, and consists of an inner reality with certain outer manifestations. The manifestations can be proved and measured, but not the inner reality, or that deeper self, which gives to the outer manifestations their unity. *
>
> By the indwelling light of this truth, I know that the world to which I belong, and which consists of an endless series of movements, has an inner truth of its own which is one, and which gives reality to the innumerable facts we know about the universe. We realize this inner truth, we experience *Ananda,* Joy, for through Joy we discover the eternal harmony of our own reality.
>
> So often we ignore the real truth of a man and only deal with surface facts about him. The man who sells things to me is, for myself, a mere fact. The man whom I employ as my servant is a bundle of certain facts, all useful in the particular facts and circumstances of my life. Through such facts I find the satisfaction of many of my needs, but no joy. for joy comes only when we realize the harmony of the Satyam, or Truth, that is in us, with the Satyam, or Truth, that is in others, and, in this case, in my servant. But with regard to our loved ones, we are directly aware of the deeper truth which is constantly manifested through them in their outer life, because with them we more easily realize a mutual affinity. Their outer activity may hold no value for our life's purposes, nay it may even be a hindrance. They have, however, an ultimate value for us in that they are, that they embody, an inner truth which is also within me.
>
> — Rabindranath Tagore : "The Philosophical Approach to Sriniketan", quoted in L.K. Elmhirst: *Rabindranath Tagore : Pioneer in Education,* John Murry, London, 1961, pp. 85-86.

The true purpose of education as Tagore advocates, is to initiate the child in the world of joy. Let the child understand and appreciate the joy of creation. Let the lesson of detachment from the self be learnt by means of joy and freedom of spirit. Let the aesthetic and the creative life of the child usher forth in the symphony of freedom and joy. The world of Nature beckons the child to participate in all her marvels of beauty and joy. Let him be allowed to solve the mystery of his own being in association with that which is realized in 'some pure moments of ecstasy' as revealed in the language of joy. In the words of Tagore,

> All the language of joy is beauty. It is necessary to note, however, that joy is not a pleasure, and beauty and mere prettiness. Joy is the outcome of detachment from self and lives in freedom of spirit. Beauty is that profound expression of reality which satisfies our hearts without any other allurements but its own ultimate value. When in some pure moments of esctasy we realize this is the world around us, we see the world, not as merely existing, but as decorated in its forms, sounds, colours and lines; we feel in our hearts that there is One who through all things proclaims : 'I have joy in my creation'.
>
> — Rabindranath Tagore : "The Creative Ideal", *Creative Unity*, Macmillan & Company Limited, London; 1962, p. 36.

Tagore allows ample freedom for pupils in education not because they lead in indisciplined life but essentially because they will learn discipline by themselves. This principle of self-discipline in education saves a learner from the rigour in the name of so-called discipline in education and also maintains a close relationship between the teacher and the learner. The climate of learning and teaching in schools becomes favourable and beneficial both to the learner and to the teacher. A free interplay of ideas and opinions between the taught and the teacher as Tagore envisages in his programmes of education at Santiniketan makes learning and teaching joyful, living and full of the promises of creativity and critical thinking.

Admittedly, the exercise of the power of imagination as well as of other powers—physical, emotional, aesthetic, spiritual and so on — depends on the fulfilment of the basic principle of education which Tagore describes as unification between life and education. Unless education is synchronized with life, it loses its real meaning and significance. Education for free developments of our inner faculties and aptitudes is, to him, more important than bookish education. In fact, he wages a war against routinized education and allows education of the child in the midst of a joyous and free atmosphere which becomes his living partner in the pursuit of education. The deep blue sky, the blood red sun, the long lost horizon, the star-studded sky at night, the stillness of silence in the vast open fields and meadows, the canvas of the trees, flowers and foliage — all add beauty and glory to the learning of a child and to any one who cares for creativity, joy and freedom as meaningful and worthwhile components in education.

True to his own being as an incomparable creative colossus, Tagore wants to involve the child in his inherent finer elements of sensitivity. That is why he emphasizes on the education of the heart along with the education of the head. Right from childhood, the learner should, according to him, enjoy a broad based avenue of efflorescence in finer sensibilities and softer visions of life. The seasonal functions and festivals in which every child actively participates make learning more interesting and realistic than undergoing day to day drudgeries in education through text-book based education. Moreover, a child is also allowed to freely participate and undergo training in performing arts like painting, drawing, music, artistic handicrafts etc. that enable him to be in tune with the joy and freedom in learning.

Tagore also encourages life-centric education for children. He allows indigenous education with creative and aesthetic modifications suited to them for efflorescence of joy and freedom. Like an uncompromising and unparalleled educator, he has written text-books and other ones of diverse disciplines for children for different age-groups so that every child is ably directed and guided towards the education of having, loving and being. His philosophy of education has broadened the mind and widened the vision of a learner who seeks freedom and joy for his *cidakas* — the sky of the mind. The world of the child is one of newer possibilities and poignance in fullness of being. Tagore always advocates that education for the child where teachers share every learner's endeavour and vision of fullness of being. Let education as he reminds time and again be emancipated from 'the dreary desert sand of dead habit'. Let the teacher and the learner pray together :

> Give me the strength lightly to bear my joys and sorrows.
> Give me the strength to make my love fruitful in service.
> Give me the strength never to disown the poor or bend my knees before insolent might.
> Give me the strength to raise my mind high above daily trifles.
> And give me the strength to surrender my strength to thy will with love.

— Rabindranath Tagore : *Gitanjali,* Macmillan

India Limited, New Delhi, 1983, No.XXXVI, p. 21.

REFERENCES

Chakrabarti, Mohit : *Philosophy of Education of Rabindranath Tagore,* Atlantic Publishers and Distributors, New Delhi, 1988.

Chakrabarti, Mohit : *Rabindranath Tagore : Diverse Dimensions,* Atlantic Publishers and Distributors, New Delhi, 1989.

Chakrabarti, Mohit : *Tagore and Education for Social Change,* Gyan Publishing House, New Delhi, 1993.

Elmhirst, L.K. : *Rabindranath Tagore : Pioneer in Education,* John Murry, London, 1961.

Tagore, Rabindranath : *The Religion of Man,* George Allen & Unwin, London, 1953.

Tagore, Rabindranath : *Creative Unity,* Macmillan & Company Limited, London, 1962.

Tagore, Rabindranath : *Siksha,* Visva-Bharati, Santiniketan, 1973.

Tagore, Rabindranath : *Gitanjali,* Macmillan India Limited, New Delhi, 1983.

9

GANDHI: Education Through Work

Of all the great educators Mahatma Gandhi holds a very distinctive position. He upholds education as a continual process of growth and development of every human being. His main concern in education is development of the inner spirit of the child, which is more important than mere rules and methods. For this, he advocates training of the mind along with training of the senses as well as of hands and feet.

Mere literacy as an aim in education for the child has, as Gandhi categorically asserts, no meaning and, therefore, no significance. True education always indicates whatever is best for him for fullness of personality. Gandhi's own exposition to this end in view of education for the child is as follows :

> By education I mean an all-round drawing out of the best in child and man — body, mind and spirit. Literacy is not the end of education nor even the beginning. It is one of the means whereby man and woman can be educated. Literacy in itself is no education. I would therefore begin the child's education by teaching it a useful handicraft and enabling it to produce from the moment it begins its training. Thus every school can be made self-supporting, the condition being that the State takes over the manufactures of this school.
>
> — M.K. Gandhi: *Harijan,* 31 July 1937.

Born at Porbandar, Gujarat, in India on October 2, 1869, Mohandas Karamchand Gandhi has his early education from his mother, a deeply devoted lady to whom his first lesson in education is one of simplicity and service through work. At school he is more concerned with the wailing of the inner self which, he thinks, can never be ameliorated by bookish education. Again, the so called discipline of school has pained him. Instead, he favours free discipline that grows in course of education through work. Later he experiments on this principle of discipline of the self through work-oriented education that is popularly known as basic education. As he believes,

> Real education consists in drawing the best out of yourself. What better book can there be than the book of humanity ?
>
> — M.K. Gandhi : *Harijan,* 30 March, 1934

To foster the spirit of humanity in education, Gandhi, therefore, evolves a new theory and practice in education. According to him,

> ... true education of the intellect can only come through a proper exercise and training of the bodily organs, e.g. hands, feet, eyes, ears, nose, etc. In other words, an intelligent use of the bodily organs in a child provides the best and quickest way of developing his intellect. But unless the development of the mind and body goes hand in hand with a corresponding awakening of the soul,the former alone would prove to be a very poor lop-sided affair. By spiritual training I mean education of the heart. A proper and all-round development of the mind therefore can take place only when it proceeds *pari passu* with the education of the physical and spiritual facalties of the child. They constitute an indivisible whole.
>
> — M.K. Gandhi, *Harijan* : 8 May, 1937

Education for spiritual training is as Gandhi strongly feels not only desirable but also mandatory. Otherwise the purposse of education for self-realization is defeated. In his own experience as a school boy he has deeply felt the absence of such education. As he obseerves.

> From my sixth or seventh-year up to my sixteenth I was at school being taught all sorts of things except religion. I may say that I failed to get from the teachers what they could have given me without any effort on their part. And yet I kept on picking up things here and there from my surroundings. The term 'religion' I am using in its broadest sense, meaning thereby self - realization or knowledge of self .

— M.K..Gandhi: *An Autobiography,* Navajivan Publishing House Ahmedabad, 1948 p. 47

Not merely the development of the brain but the development of the hand and the soul is what Gandhi advocates in education. Otherwise, education remains incomplete. As he categorically states,

> I would develop in the child his hands, his brain, and his soul. The hands have almost atrophied. The soul has been altogether ignored

— R. K.Prabhu and U.R. Rao (Compiled); *The Mind of Mahatma Gandhi,* Oxford University Press, 1945, p. 161.

Elsewhere, Gandhi makes a simpler exposition on the importance of education of the hand:

> The utterly false idea that intelligence can be developed only through book reading should give place to the truth that the quickest development of the mind be achieved by artisans work being learnt in a scientific manner. True development of the mind commences immediately the apprentice is taught at every step why a particular manipulation of the hand or a tool is required .

— M.K. Gandhi: *Harijan,* January, 1937

To liberate the learner from heaps of books, Gandhi emphasizes on the training to think. This enables the learner to discriminate between right and wrong, good and evil and so on. Thus the learner develops self-respect through self-assessment which constitutes a vital part in the practice of education. As Gandhi significantaly points out.

> Pupils should know to discriminate what should be received and what rejected. It is the duty of the teacher to teach, the pupils discrimination. If we go on taking in indiscriminately we would be no better than machines. We are thinking, knowing being and we must in this period distinguish truth from untruth, sweet from bitter language, clean from unclean things and so on. But the student's path today is strewn with more difficulties than the one of distinguishing good from bad things .The *rishis* taught their pupils without books. They only gave them a few mantras which the pupils

> treasured in their memories and translated in practical life. The present day student has to live in the midst of heaps of books sufficient to choke him .
>
> — M.K Gandhi: *Young India,* 29 January, 1925

The goal of education as Gandhi thinks is not mere literacy deplorable as it is but to enable pupils to exercise courage, strength and virtue. These are the fundamental components of spiritual education .But how to impart spiritual training? Gandhi's experience in the Tolstoy Farm as a teacher gives the appropriate answer:

> The spiritual training of the boys was a much more difficult matter than their physical and mental training. I relied little on religious books for the training of the spirit. Of course, I believed that every student should be acquainted with the elements of his own religion and have a general knowledge of his own scriptures and therefore I provided for such knowledge as best as I could. But that, to my mind, was part of the intellectual training. Long before I undertook the education of the youngsters of the Tolstoy Farm I had realised that the training of spirit is to build character and to enable one to work towards a knowledge of God and self realisation. And I held that this was an essential fact of the training of the young and that all training without culture of the spirit was of no use and might be even harmful.
>
> — M.K.Gandhi: *An Autobiography,* Navajivan Publishing House, Ahmedabad, 1927, p. 149.

That spiritual education by means of books is of no value is again and again reminded be Gandhi .His own suggestion is to exercise the spirit inherent in oneself. That is why the teacher plays a very significant part in spiritual education. He must serve as a living example with his own life and character to impart such education. As a teacher, he spells out his own strategy:

> I made the children memorize and recite hymns and read to them from books on moral training . But that was far from satisfying me. As I came into closer contact with them I saw that it was that through books that one could impart training of the spirit. Just as physical training was to be imparted through physical exercise, even so the training of the spirit was possible only through the exercise of the

spirit. And the exercise of the spirit entirely depended on the life and character of the teacher. The teacher had always to be mindful of his P's and Q's whether he was in the midst of his boys or not.

— *Ibid*

Education as Gandhi highlights, is a process of self-purification. The more one purifies oneself in thought, more deed and action the more is one hallowed with the inherent spirit of education. The role of a learner in the pursuit of education is to lead a life of purity and simplicity like a *brahmachari*. Whatever sound education he aims at must, therefore be based on a sound moral character ably guarded by poignance of purity . As Gandhi remarks .

Purity of personal life is the one indespensable condition for building a sound education. And my meeting with thousands of students and the correspondence which I continuously have with students in which they pour out innermost feelings and take me into their confidence, show me quite clearly that there is much left to be desired. I am sure that all of you understand thoroughly what I mean. In our languages there is a beautiful word equivalent for the word student, that is *brahmachari*. And I hope you know what the word *brahmachari* means. It means searcher after God in the least possible time . And all the great religions of the world however much they may differ, are absolutely one of this fundamental thing that no man or woman with an inpure heart can possibly appear before the Great White Throne. All our learning or recitation of the vedas, correct knowledge of Sanskrit, Latin, Greek and what not will avail us nothing if they do not enable us to cultivate absolute purity of heart. The end of all knowledge must be building up of character.

— M.K.Gandhi: *Young India*, 8 September, 1927

The 'culture of the heart' or character-building is the primary end in view of Gandhian philosophy of education . It is this cullture which Gandhi emphasizes upon introducing right from the school stage where children learn though freedom and joy. The teacher is there to infuse in them the spirit of truth, goodness, and beauty. The teacher is also there to orient them in the service of others in order to serve themselves best .

A radical and revolutionary in education, Gandhi makes a daring experiment in co-education based on self-restraint and self-discipline

Pupils under such experimentations learn how to honour one another and thus glorify themselves with the spirit of self-honour and self-steem. Moreover, children also learn the education of simplicity by leading a conjoint, communicated, simple and honest life amidst austerity. They cultivate the finer values and nobler principles of life by exercising tolerance, sympathy and benevolence in thought and action .

The following is an interesting account of how Gandhi as a teacher has imparted the education for moral and spiritual efflorescence:

> The heterogeneous class that fell to Gandhi's lot contained pupils of all ages from boys and girls of about seven years of age to young men of twenty and young girls of twelve. As the principal part of the teaching, he follows the method of narrating or reading to his pupils interesting stories. No text-books were used in this school. In education he gave the first place to the culture of the heart or the building of character. Corporal punishment strictly forbidden . Gandhi believed that the training of the spirit was only possible through the exercise of the spirit. And the exercise of the spirit entirely depended on the life and character of the teacher. Only on one occasion Gandhi punished a pupil with a ruler, trembling as he struck the erant pupil.
>
> His experiment on co-education at Tolstoy Farm was a daring one. He sent young boys reputed to be mischievous and the innocent young girls to bathe at the same spot at the same time. He fully explained the duty of self-restraint to his pupils. The bathers went in a body and solitude was always avoided and he usually was present at the spring.
>
> Gandhi slept in an open veranda, and the boys and girls would spread themselves around him. There was no cot on the farm; all slept on the floor. For bed every one was given two blankets, one for spreading and the other for covering purpose and wooden pillow. The experiment made from a belief that boys and girls could thus live together without harm did not always work very smoothly.
>
> Many observed the *Ekadashi* fast on the farm, and some kept *Chaturmas.* To keep company with the Muslim inmates the rest had only one meal a day in the evening during the *Ramzan* days. All assisted each other in their respective religious observances. The fasts were also considered an aid in self-restraint.
>
> — D.G. Tendulkar: *Mahatma,* Publications Division, Ministry of Information and

Broadcasting Government of India, Vol. I, pp. 118-120.

The concept of the whole man as Gandhi seeks and disseminates in course of education through work is essentially geared to eliminate intellectual dissipation. The education of the child, as he advocates, should have comparative approach to harmonious development of physical, mental and emotional sensibilities. Therefore, when he speaks of basic education, his primary concern is to synchronize education with work, and work with worship. In his words,

> Supposing he (the child) is set to some useful occupation like spinning, carpentry, agriculture, etc. for his education and in that connection is given a thorough comprehensive knowledge relating to the theory of the various operations that he is to perform and the use and construction of the tools that he would be wielding. He would not only develop a fine, healthy body but also a sound, vigorous intellect that is not merely acedemic but is firmly rooted in and is tested from day to day by experience. His intellectual education would include a knowledge of mathematics and the various sciences that are useful for an intelligent and efficient exercise of his evocation. If to this is added literature by way of recreation, all-round education in which the intellect, the body and the spirit have all full play and develop together into a natural, harmonious whole. Man is neither mere intellect, nor the gross animal body, nor the heart or soul alone. A proper and harmonious combination of all the three is required for the making of the whole man, and constitutes the true economics of education.

— M. K. Gandhi : *Basic Education,* Navajivan Publishing House, Ahmedabad, 1956, pp. 11-12.

The success of the Wardha Scheme of education and its wide acceptance by educationists make Gandhi more interested and hopeful in bringing about a worthwhile revolution in education through work. As a matter of fact, his own reaction to the popularity of the scheme and emphasis on education of the child for creative, emotional and aesthetic developments necessitate a re-thinking :

I am grateful that so many educationists have blessed the new

> scheme. There have been critics also, but when I launched the scheme I did not know that it would appeal to anyone beyond the circle of my co-workers. When I consider the masses of India and the masses situated as they are, I could not think of any other of education. With them work must precede anything else, and the concern of an educationist is to make that work educative. Let every child feel that he creates something for use and also expands his mind and heart therethrough.
>
> — M.K. Gandhi: *Harijan*, 11 December, 1937.

The education of excellence of each individual for the greater goodness and excellence of the society as a whole is the fundamental objective of the Gandhian philosophy of education. Let the mind of every individual, as Gandhi thinks, be enriched with the education of goodness. Let him be allowed to exercise his power of individuality enlightened with the spirit of wisdom to usher forth a better enlightened global society. As a true sociologist, he emphasizes on efflorescence of individuality by means of education first and then on synchronization between the individual and the society. His principle of education as revealed in his principle of *Sarvodaya* is primarily based on education for total development of each individual. Thus as an educational sociologist, he makes a significant departure from others :

> Men on the Left put the interest of society first and make the individual subserve to society. Those who on the Right make the individual too important and deny any social obligation. There is a distortion of reality. The individual and society are not two separate entities; they are but two sides of the same coin. * * * I am deeply aware of the importance of the individual. The individaul mind is the birthplace of all that is new, all that is good. Through him alone it spreads in society; he is its vehicle. *Sarvodaya* gives the greatest importance to the full development and well-being of the individual * * * *Sarvodaya* does not believe in the doctrine for achieving the greatest good of the greatest number * * * *Sarvodaya* is the well-being of everyone. It believes that there can be no conflict between the real good of one person and that of another.
>
> — Horace Alexander: *Consider India,* Asia Publishing House, Bombay, 1961, pp. 144-145.

For a real regeneration of the society, Gandhi introduces the spinning wheel as a craft education for self-honour and self-reliance. The daily routine -work in spinning at school will enable children to understand and appreciate the socio-intellectual value of spinning which contributes a lot to individual and social development. Gandhi further spells out the education of the spinning wheel as follows :

> A cause is often greater than man. Certainly the spinning wheel is greater than myself. With it, in my opinion, is mixed up the well-being of the whole mass of Indian humanity. The pupils should, therefore, learn something about the deep poverty of the masses. They should have an ocular demonstration of some villages that are crumbling down to pieces. They should know the population of India. They should know the vast extent of this peninsula and they should know what it is that all the millions can do to add to their scanty resources. They should learn to identify themselves with the poor and the downtrodden in the land. They should be taught to deny themselves, so far as possible, the things that the poorest cannot take. Then they will understand the virtue of head-spinning. It will then survive any shock including disillusionment about myself. The cause of the spinning wheel is too great and too good to have to rest on mere hero-worship.
>
> — D.G. Tendulkar : *Mahatma*, Publications Division, Ministry of Information and Broadcasting, Government of India, Vol. II, pp. 223-224.

The concept of 'the whole education' as Gandhi spells out, clearly explains why he wants to introduce his own basic education programmes in schools. His emphasis on involving the child in learning handicrafts is in tune with this wholeness in education. As he observes,

> The scheme that I wish to place is not the teaching of some handicrafts side by side with so-called liberal education. I want that the whole education should be imparted through some handicrafts or industry. It might be objected that in the middle ages only handicrafts were taught to the students; but the occupational training, then, was far from serving on educational purpose. The crafts were taught only for the sake of the crafts without any attempt to develop the intellect as well. In this age those born in certain professions had

> forgotten them, had taken to clerical careers and were lost to countryside. The remedy lies in imparting the whole art and science of a craft through practical training and then through imparting the whole education.
>
> — Mahatma Gandhi: *Harijan,* 30 October, 1937.

Why does Gandhi give importance to the training of the hands in the education of the child ? The answer lies in the fact that true education brings forth music in life, and to understand and appreciate that music which is not available in the stereotyped pattern of bookish education should be the fundamental objective of education. As Gandhi categorically observes,

> If I were a poet, I could write poetry on the possibilities of the five fingers. And why should you think that the mind is everything and the hands and the feet are nothing? Those who don't train their hands, who go through the ordinary rut of education, lack 'music' in their life. All their faculties are not trained. Mere book knowledge does not interest the child, so as to hold his attention fully. The brain gets weary of mere words, and the child's mind begins to wander. The hand does the thing it ought not to do, the eye sees the things it ought not to see, and the ear hears the things it ought not to hear, and they do not do, see or hear, respectively, what they ought to. They are not taught to make the right choice and so their education often proves their ruin.
>
> — D.G. Tendulker: *Mahatma,* Publications Division, Ministry of Information and Broadcasting, Government of India, Vol. V, p.43.

The education of the child in awareness for the development of body, mind and spirit as Gandhi envisaged is an integral part of the education of love. For this, the education for the quest of Truth and Non-violence is essential. How to impart the education of Truth, and Non-violence ? Gandhi's answer lies in following the fundamental principle of work as worship which stands for all experiments with Truth and Non-violence. He speaks on character-building as an essential objective of education which in particular is an unending devotion to Truth and Non-violence. The exercise of moral force in every sphere of life and activity heralds and brightens education as a positive exposure in Truth-force or the key force of human excellence that embraces one and all even under trying circumstances. The child, therefore, necessitiates a favourable and stimulating avenue of developing the moral, spiritual and aesthetic sensibilities already in him beyond the horizon of bookish education. Such an education in theory and practice by the child ensures a broadened vision and widened approach to mankind in course of pursuing Truth and Non-violence that acts as a soul-force.

As a pioneer in education, Gandhi is more interested in fullness of education in all respects and fullness of man than in education as an exercise of the intellect alone. A comprehensive development of the child cannot but incorporate the education of love, sympathy and humanity, truth, self-service and devotion to work. For such education, teachers play the most vital role in inspiring and enkindling every child to make a real adventure into the world of erudition and work, learning and devotion to Truth, Beauty and Goodness.

The role of the teacher is best justified in terms of Gandhi's own exposition as a teacher:

> It is impossible for a teacher situated miles away to affect the spirit of the pupils by his way of living. It would be idle for me, if I were a liar, to teach boys to tell the truth. A cowardly teacher would never succeed in making the boys valiant, and a stranger to self-restraint could never teach his pupils the value of self-restraint. I saw, therefore, that I must be an eternal object-lesson to the boys and girls living with me. They thus become my teachers and I learnt I must be good and live straight, if only for their sakes I may say that the increasing discipline and restraint I imposed on myself at Tolstoy Farm was mostly due to those wards of mine.
>
> — M.K. Gandhi : *An Autobiography,* Navajivan Publishing House, Ahmedabad, 1926, p.418.

The education of the child for emancipation of individuality, as Gandhi advocates, is the primary need of the hour. And, for this, teachers must come forward with a dedicated mission and untiring zeal to understand, evaluate and thereby re-orient education to mobilize and enrich the finer sense of honour and individuality with which he is gifted right from birth. To emancipate the best from the child in education, Gandhi banks upon the right type of teachers, and so suggests :

> We have to fall back upon the voluntary assistance of the teachers but when I look for teachers, they are very few, especially, the teachers of the type wanted, in order to draw the best from the children through understanding, through studying their individuality and then putting the child on its own resources, as it were on its honour. From my own experience of hundreds, I was going to say thousands, of children—I know that they have perhaps a finer sense of honour than you and I have.
>
> — D.G. Tendulkar : *Mahatma,* Publications Division, Ministry of Information and Broadcasting, Government of India, Vol. III, p. 137.

Admittedly, Gandhi brings about a redical approach to education of the child from fourfold avenue of emancipation of consciousness by means of work :

(i) To the child, education should be as natural and realistic as possible. In order to be so, it must be an indigenous one that introduces the child with down-to-earth and life-centric experiences;

(ii) The education of the child demands for its spontaneity an atmosphere of freedom ably nursled in the mother-tongue;

(iii) The education of the child should incorporate the principles of self-reliance and self-discipline which always stimulate him to endear work as worship; and

(iv) True education should always be a fillip to the child in character-building. This will lead to continual exercise and enrichment of inner excellence.

From a study of the four-fold avenue of emancipation of consciousness as Gandhi highlights in his educational thoughts and experiments, it is evident that his philosophy of education is attuned to the great saying of the *Upanishad : ah noh bhadra kratava yantu visvata* — let noble thoughts come to us from every direction.

As an educational humanist, Gandhi glorifies the vision of man whom he adores as *Naranarayan* or *Daridranarayan* — God embodied in man or God as represented by the poor. The first education for the child should, according to him, be the lesson of goodness for one and all. Let the child be saved from all narrowness of thought and action. Let the lesson of love for all be the guiding force in the education of the child.

Education, to Gandhi, is never an end in itself but a means to an end. For this, he is always against education as a static force but considers it a means for the beyonding of all knowledge and wisdom. As a mystic *par excellence* in education, his end-in-view is hallowed with the principle of progress or advancement unending but thrilling, incomplete but stimulating—*Charaiveti:* March on.

The education of love and sympathy that Gandhi launches in his programme of basic education translates the spirit of religion of global relationship : *Vasudhaiva Kutumvakam*. More often misunderstood than not, the lesson of religion that Gandhi wants to impart by sincerely introducting the spirit of non-violence is the religion of man endaring man. And this religion awaits efflorescence in the learner right from the school stage. The essence of spiritualism finds a new language in the control of the self that harbours only upon Truth.

The future of man the excellent awaits, as Gandhi reminds us time and again, the radical change in the pattern of education where the child hormonizes all the inherent qualities of the head and the hand, the heart and the brain for transvaluation of values. The education of transcendence as an ardent endeavour as Gandhi aims at in his educational philosophy is long overdue in our present day ukase in education.

Do we respond even now ?

REFERENCES

Alexander, Horace : *Consider India,* Asia Publishing House, Bombay, 1961.

Chakrabarti, Mohit : *Gandhian Mysticism,* Atlantic Publishers and Distributors, New Delhi, 1989.

Chakrabarti, Mohit : *The Gandhian Dimensions of Education,* Daya Publishing House, New Delhi, 1990.

Chakrabarti, Mohit : *Gandhian Aesthetics,* Atlantic Publishers and Distributors, New Delhi, 1990.

Chakrabarti, Mohit : *Gandhian Humanism,* Concept Publishing Company, New Delhi, 1992.

Chakrabarti, Mohit : *Gandhian Spiritualism,* Concept Publishing Company, New Delhi, 1993.

Gandhi, M.K. : *Harijan.*

Gandhi, M.K. : *Young India.*

Gandhi, M.K. : *An Autobiography,* Navajivan Publishing House, Ahmedabad, 1948.

Gandhi, M.K. : *Basic Education,* Navajivan Publishing House, Ahmedabad, 1956.

Prabhu, R.K. & Rao U. R. (Compiled) : *The Mind of Mahatma Gandhi,* Oxford University Press, London, 1945.

Tendulkar, D.G. : *Mahatma,* Publications Division, Ministry of Information and Broadcasting, Government of India.

10

VIVEKANANDA : Vibrant Education

Education is an unending force — eternal, intrinsic, bouyant and vibrant. It is a force that storms the mighty Himalayas and brings forth a calmness of mind all passions spent. It enkindles the lamp of askance and enquiry as it were and allows man the endless learner 'to follow knowledge' as Tennyson's Ulysses does, 'like a sinking star'. To Swami Vivekananda, the role of a learner in education is always guided by the great saying: *Uttisthata Yagrata prapya varan nivodhata* — 'Arise, awake, and stop not till the goal is reached'.

Believing that all knowledge is inherent in one's own soul, Swami Vivekananda makes the teacher aware of an essential fact that the child learns himself, teaches himself, turns himself and transcends himself. Education is, therefore, simply a manifestation of inherent perfection. It is a continual process of discovery of the 'man' in man, the 'man' in the child, the man divine as Vivekananda poignantly observes.

> Knowledge is inherent in man, no knowledge comes from outside; it is all inside. What we say a man 'knows' should, in strict psychological language, be what he 'discovers' or unveils! What a man 'learns' is really what he 'discovers' by taking the cover off his own soul which is a mine of infinite knowledge. We say Newton discovered gravitation. Was it sitting anywhere in a corner waiting for him? It was in his own mind; the time came and he found it out. All knowledge that the world has ever received comes from the mind. The external world is only the suggestion, the occasion, which sets you to study your own mind. The falling of an apple gave the suggestion to Newton, and he studied his own mind. We rearranged all the previous links of thoughts in the mind and discovered a new link among them, which we call the law of gravitation. It was not in

the apple nor in anything but in the centre of the earth.

— *The Complete Work of Swami Vivekananda,* Mayavati Memorial Edition, 1962, Vol. I, p. 28.

The education that Vivekananda wants to impart among learners is the education of the discovery of the self. Such a discovery encompasses knowledge and power that are withing oneself. The role of the learner, as he believes, is to manifest the knowledge and power within himself. As he observes,

> All knowledge and power are within. What we call powers, secrets of Nature, and force are all within. All knowledge comes from the human soul. Man manifests knowledge, discovers it within himself, which is, pre-existing, through eternity.

— *Ibid,* p. 422.

Like an incomparable auto-educationist, Vivekananda encourages self-education. He reminds us that a child learns himself. He teaches himself. The role of the teacher is to help him, to find out the true way of education himself. Like a plant, the child develops his own nature of manifestation. In such manifestation the role of the teacher in not to teach as such but to lend a helping hand, if necessary, in terms of guidance and protection. Vivekananda reminds the teacher of the role he should play as follows :

> The child also teaches itself. But you can help it to go forward in its own way. What you can do is not of a positive nature but negative. You can take away the obstacles, and knowledge comes out of own nature—Loosen the soil a little so that it may come out easily. Put a hedge round it; see that it is not killed by anything.

— *Ibid,* Vol. IV, p. 55.

Elsewhere, Vivekananda points out the limitations of the so-called teaching that encroaches upon the child's personality :

The teacher spoils everything by thinking that he is teaching. Within man is all knowledge, and it requires only an awakening, and that much is the work of the teacher. We have only to do so much for the boys that they may learn to apply their own intellect to the proper use of their hands, legs, ears and eyes.

— Ibid, Vol. V, p. 366.

In educating the child, Vivekananda harps on positive thinking. He points out the drawbacks of negative thoughts that eat up the very promises of poignance in a child and stimulate whatever acts as a positive force in the advancement of learning. In his words,

> We should give positive ideas. Negative thoughts only weaken men. Do you not find that where parents are constantly taking their sons to read and write, telling them that they will never learn anything and calling them fools and so forth, the latter do actually turn out to be so in many cases? If you speak kind words to them and encourages them, they are bound to improve in time. If you can give them positive ideas, people will grow up to be men and learn to stand on their own legs. In language and literature, in poetry and arts, in every thing we must point out not the mistakes that people are making in their thoughts and actions, but the way in which they will be able to do these things better.

— *Ibid,* Vol. VII, p.170.

When Vivekananda speaks of positive education he means that kind of education in which one discovers oneself. It is that education which allows one to enter deep into the soul of education — ' life-building, man-making, character-making, assimilation of ideas'. As such, education eliminates bare information and prepares one to bring out strength of character, a spirit of philanthropy and the courage of a lion. Denouncing education as equivalent to information, he significantly remarks,

> Education is not the amount of information that is put into your brain and runs riot there, undigested all your life. We must have life-building, man-making, character-making, assimilation of ideas. It you have assimilated five ideas and made them your life and character, you have more education than any man who has got by heart a whole library. If education were identical with information, the libraries would be the greatest sages in the world and encyclpaedias of the Rishis.

—*Ibid,* Vol. III, p. 302.

Pointing out the appalling condition of education wrongly imparted in the country, Vivekananda warned against education that is ignorant of others in and around us:

> Getting by heart the thought of others in a foreign language and stuffing your brian with them and taking some university degrees, you consider yourself educated. Is this education? What is the goal of your education ? Either a clerkship, or being a lawyer, or at the most a Deputy Magistrate, which is another form of clerkship — isn't that all ? What good will it do you or the country at large ? Open your eyes and see what a piteous cry for food is rising in the land of Bharata proverbial for its food. Will your education fulfil this want?
>
> —*Ibid,* Vol. VII, p. 182.

As regards the method of education, Vivekananda emphasizes on concentration of mind which he considers a key point to success in attainment of true knowledge. In his own words,

> From the lowest man to the highest Yogi, all have to use the same method to attain knowledge. The chemist who works in laboratory, concentrates all the powers of his mind, brings them into one focus, and throws them on the elements; the elements stand analysed, and thus his knowledge comes. The astronomer concentrates the powers of his mind and brings them into one focus; and he throws them on the objects through his telescope, and stars and systems roll forward and give up their secrets to him. So it is in every case; within the professor in his chair, the student with his book, with every man who is working to know.
>
> —*Ibid.,* Vol. II, pp. 390-391.

Elsewhere, Vivekananda speaks about the essence of education harping on the same principle of concentration of mind :

> To me the very essence of education is concentration of mind, not the collection of facts. If I had to do my education once again, I would not study facts at all. I would develop the power of concentration and detachment, and then with a perfect instrument,

collelct facts at will.

— *Ibid,* Vol, VI, p. 38-39.

To instil the spirit of reverence in every child, as Vivekananda suggests, is to beckon the spirit of self-respect that holds the core of education. This is, indeed, his own mission of life :

> To preach the doctrine of Shraddha or genuine faith is the mission of my life. Let me repeat to you that this faith is one of the most potent factors of humanity. First have faith in yourselves. Know that one may be a little bubble and another may be a mountain-high wave, yet behind both the bubble and the wave there is the infinite ocean.

— *Ibid,* Vol. III, p. 444.

A true recognition, right from the beginning of education of the child, of the infinite ocean in very human being is the *sine qua non* of education for fullness. Vivekananda calls this type of education the education for recognition of the innate powers in every human being and advises on imparting that type of education to children :

> The infinite occan is the background of me as well as you. Mine also is that infinite ocean of life, of power, of spirituality as well as yours. Therefore, my brethren, teach this life-saving, great, ennobling, grand doctrine to your children even from their very birth.

— *Ibid,* p. 376.

The education for building up characters and manifesting the real resplendant ever-pure nature in oneself is, as Vivekananda observes, the primary objective of education. As such, to strengthen the will-force in oneself is to eleminate darkness of errors and ignorance and effulge light of fullness and perfection. Vivekananda makes a fine analysis on this point:

> We commit mistakes because we are weak and we are weak because we are ignorant. Who makes us ignorant ? We ourselves. We put our hands over our eyes and weep that it is dark. Take the hands away and there is light. The light exists always for us, the self-effulgent nature of the human soul. Do you not hear what modern scientific

men say ? What is the cause of evolution ? Desire, the animal wants to do something but does not find the environment favourable, and therefore develops a new body. Who develops it ? The animal itself: its will. Continue to exercise your will and it will take you higher. The will is almighty. If it is almighty, you may say : why cannot I do everything ? But you are thinking only of your little self. Look back on yourself from the state of the amoeba to the human being; who made all that ? Your own will. Can you deny that it is almighty ? That which has made you come up so high, can make you go higher still. What you want is character, strenghening of the will.

—*Ibid,* Vol. II, pp. 356-357

Education for an ideal development of personality necessitates, as Vivekananda advocates, training in man-making. The education of the inner man as he strongly feels, is long overdue. Here book knowledge, therefore, will not do. Education must be a dynamic force that effulges and emancipates the inner man—the man who continually grows. As Vivekananda categorically states,

> The ideal of all education, all training, should be this man-making. But, instead of that, we are always trying to polish up the outside. The end and aim of all training is to make the man grow. The man who influences, who throws his magic, as it were, upon his fellow beings, is a dynamo of power, and when that man is ready, he can do anything and everything he likes; that personality put upon anything will make it work.
>
> Now we see that though this is a fact, no physical laws that we know of will explain this. How can we explain it by chemical and physical knowledge? How much of oxygen, hydrogen, carbon — how many molecules in different positions and how many cells, etc., can explain this mysterious personality? And we still see, it is a fact, and not only that, it is the real man; and it is that man that influences, moves his fellow-beings and passes out, and his intellect and books works are but traces left behind.

— *Ibid,* Vol. II, pp. 14-15.

As pioneer in education, Vivekananda determines and suggests certain conditions for a student to be a student in the true sense of the term. In his words:

> The conditions necessary for the taught are purity, a real thirst after knowledge, and perseverance. Purity in thought, speech and act is absolutely necessary. As for thirst after knowledge, it is an old law that we all get whatever we want. None of us can get anything other than what we fix out hearts upon. There must be a continuous struggle, a constant fight, an unremitting grapling with our lower nature, till the higher want is actually felt and victory is achieved. The student who sets out with such a spirit of perseverance will surely find success at last.
>
> — *Ibid,* Vol. III, pp. 102-103.

The qualities of a student as suggested by Vivekananda go a long way in orienting life towards purity and perfection. Let the student be baptised with that religious education that paves newer avenues of possessing and nursling strength within him. This will enable him to have the true concept of religion which stands for goodness. This will also enable him to identify and analyse all weakness and selfishness. This, then, is the fundamental characteristic of all religious education. The discovery of strength within oneself leads to purity and perfection. Vivekananda encourages that type of religious education which ensures this discovery of strengh - *'So' ham'*—within every student. As his vibrant words remind us of the truth:

> All sins and all evil can be summed up in that one word : weakness. It is weakness that is the motive power in all evil doing. It is weakness that is the source of all selfishness. It is weakness that makes man injure others. Let them all know what they are, let them repeat day and night what they are: *'So' ham'.* Let them suck it in with their mother's milk, this idea of strength — I am He ! This is to be first heard; and then let them think of it; and out of that thought will proceed works, such as the world has never seen.
>
> — *Ibid,* Vol. III, p. 426

Admittedly, to strengthen one's mind with Truth is the most prized lesson in religion. Children should be taught to discover Truth to prove their inner strength from every aspect — physical, mental, spiritual. Every lesson on religion should, therefore, be geared to the discovery of Truth. Such a discovery will make a learner fearless and cultivate the spirit of strength so sadly lacking in our system of education. Elucidating on the true concept of strength that a learner should always cultivate heart and soul, Vivekananda observes :

> Strength, strength is what the Upanishads speaks to me from every page. It is the only literature in the world, where you find the word 'Abhih',? 'Fearless', used again and again. In no other scripture in the world is this adjective applied either to God or man. And in my mind rises from the past the vison of the great emperor of the West, Alexander the Great, and I see as it were in a picture the great monarch standing on the banks on the Indus, talking to, perhaps naked, stark naked, sitting upon a block of stone, and the Emperor astonished at his wisdom tempting him with gold and honour, to come over to Greece. And this man smiles at his gold and smiles at his temptations, and refuses. And then the Emperor standing in his authority as Emperor says,'I will kill you if you do not come, and the man bursts into a laugh, and says, ' You never told such a falsehood in your life as you tell, just now. Who can kill me ? For I am spirit unborn and undecaying'. That is strength !
>
> — *Ibid,* pp. 237-238

The lesson on the true concept of religion as Vivekananda significantly asserts, is learnt not through definition but through realisation. As such, all books on religion from which a learner learns, serve as a means and are never the last words on religion. Let every learner experience by himself and along with others the concept of religion in action, for it is not a static but a dynamic, living force that pulsates to prove his worth as a being in becoming. As Vivekananda reminds us,

> Temples and Churches, books and forms are simply the kindergarten of religion, to make the spiritual child strong enough to take the higher steps. Religion is not in doctrines or dogmas nor in intellectual argumentation. It is being and becoming. It is realisation.
>
> — *Ibid,* Vol. II, p. 43

To impart religious education, Vivekananda emphasizes on teaching pupils how to cultivate the heart. Mere intellectual education makes education incomplete in the sense that the lesson of cultivation of heart remains absent. If there is no synchronization between the heart and brain, education fails to play its true role in the ascent of man which is true religion. Vivekananda simplifies this point on reorienting intellectual training with religious and spiritual one as follows :

> We may be the most intellectual people the world ever saw and yet we may not come to God at all. On the other hand, irreligious men have been produced from the most intellectual training. It is one of the evils of Western civilization — intellectual education alone without taking care of the heart. It only makes men ten times more selfish. When there is conflict between the heart and the brain, let the heart be followed. It is the heart which takes one to the highest place, which intellect can never reach. It goes beyond the intellect and reaches what is called inspiration.
>
> — *Ibid.* Vol. I, p.412.

The initial and all important lesson on religious education is, therefore, the lesson of keeping wide open 'the window of heart', as Vivekananda makes us aware, and allow all religion to embrace goodness in mankind. The altruistic approach to religious education will enable the pupil to be more responsive to the inherent truth of all religion that stands for the ascent of man and teaches the lesson of excellence in thought and action. This will also teach him how to broaden the mind and widen the outlook, how to embrace the essence of all religion that brings forth true wisdom and humanity. To march on from the present to the hallowed days of future awaits a certain sense of consciousness within every learner, which can be derived from a learning of the books on religion, and that religion stands as a supreme force in enkindling the spirit of humanism in him. Vivekananda's own approach to such type of religious education elucidates the point best :

> I accept all religions that were in the past and and worship them in whatever form they worship Him. I shall go to the mosque of the Mohammedan; I shall enter the Christian's church and kneel before the crucifix. I shall enter the Buddhistic temple, where I shall take refuge in Buddha and in his Law. I shall go into the forest and sit down in meditation with the Hindu, who is trying to see the light which enlightens the heart of everyone.
>
> Not only shall I do all these but I shall keep my heart open for all that may come in the future. Is God's book finished ? Or is it still a continuous revelation going on? It is a marvellous book - these spiritual revelations of the world. The *Bible,* the *Vedas,* the *Koran* and all other secred books are but so many pages, and an infinite

> number of pages remain yet to be unfolded. Let us take in all that has been in the past, enjoy the light of the present and open every window of the heart for all that will come in the future. Salutation to all the prophets of the past, to all the great ones of the present and to all that are to come in the future.
>
> — *Ibid,* Vol. II, pp. 373-374.

Vivekananda teaches the lesson of self-renunciation which considers to be the fundamental objective of education. Like a true educational philosopher, unparalleled and incomparable, he insists on imparting the lesson of selfless service which is the essence of education. He, therefore, advises :

> Ask nothing; want nothing in return. Give what you have to give; it will come back to you—but do not think of that now. It will come back multiplied thousandfold - but the attention must not be on that. You have the power to give; give, and there it ends. Learn that the whole of life is giving, that nature will force you to give. So, give willingly. Sooner or later you will have to give up. You come into life to accumulate. With clenched hands, you want to take. But nature puts a hand on your throat and makes your hands open. Whether you will it or not, you have to give. * * * Ask, therefore, nothing in return; but the more you give, the more will come to you.
>
> — *Ibid,* Vol. I, p. 7.

As regards education of the masses, Vivekananda prescribes awakening of the spirit of consciousness. This is prossible through awakening of individuality. The education geared to the awakening of individuality goes a long way in the advancement of mass consciousness. In his words,

> The only service to be done for our lower classes is to give them education to develop their individuality. They are to be given ideas. Their eyes are to be opened to what is going on in the world around them, and then they will work out their own salvation. Every nation, every man and every woman must work out their own salvation. Give them ideas—that is the only help they require and then the rest must follow as effect. Ours is to put the chemicals together, the crystallization comes in the law of nature.

—*Ibid,* Vol. IV, p. 362.

The golden strategy for dissemination of mass education as propounded by Vivekananda is unique for two reasons. First, it is down-to-earth and does not call forth any particular theory or dogma in the name of pedagogy. Secondly, the tools or devices, applied for mass education are very simple but very effective. As he strongly suggests,

> If the poor boy cannot come to education, education must go to him. There are thousands of single-minded, self-sacrificing *Sannyasins* in our own country, going from village to village, teaching religion. If some of them can be organised as teachers of secular things also, they will go from place to place, from door to door, not only preaching but teaching also. Suppose two of these men go to a village in the evening with a camera, a globe, some maps etc., they can teach a great deal of astronomy and geography to the ignorant. By telling stories about different nations, they can give the poor a hundred times more information through the ear than they get in a lifetime through books.

— *Ibid,* Vol. VI, p. 489.

Undeniably, the teacher holds a very responsible position in imparting education to the learners. The three essential qualifications for him, as Vivekananda emphasizes, are :

(a) He should have a firm grip over 'the spirit of the scriptures'.
(b) He must be pure in character and personality.
(c) He must always be above any kind of selfish motive.

Real education always encompasses a real understanding between the teacher and the taught. If the teacher rises up to the occasion of transference and is not merely satisfied with stimulation of the intellectual and other faculities already existent in the taught, he justifies his assignment as a teacher correctly and appropraitely. A natural concern for genuine sympathy on the part of a teacher for his pupil is what is needed most in education. As Vivekananda characteristically remarks,

> The only true teacher is he who can convert himself, as it were, into a thousand persons at a moment's notice. The true teacher is he who can immediately come down to the level of the student, and transfer

his soul and see through and understand through his mind. Such a teacher can really teach and none else.

— *Ibid*, Vol. IV, p. 183.

Who differs ?

REFERENCES

Chakrabarti, Mohit : *Swami Vivekananda : A Study on Aesthetics*, Atlantic Publishers and Distributors, New Delhi, 1993.

Vivekananda, Swami : *The Complete Works of Swami Vivekananda*, Advaita Ashrama, Calcutta, Mayavati Memorial Edition, 1962.

INDEX